THE JEWEL OF
KNOWLEDGE

KEYS TO THE KINGDOM SERIES
POCKET EDITION

THIS BOOK SHOULD NOT BE LEFT ACCESSIBLE, IN CLEAR VIEW, OR SHARED CASUALLY WITH OTHERS

Published from
Mardukite Borsippa HQ, San Luis Valley, Colorado
Mardukite Academy & Systemology Society
for spiritual or philosophical purposes only

THE JEWEL OF KNOWLEDGE

Systemology
Advanced Training Course
Manual #3

As presented by Joshua Free
to the Systemology Society

THE JOSHUA FREE IMPRINT
JFI PUBLICATIONS

ISBN : 978-1-961509-49-8

This manual is restricted to students on
The Systemology Advanced Training Course
that have already completed the
"Pathway to Ascension" Professional Course

References to prerequisite material:
"The Secret of Universes" (AT #1)
"Games, Goals & Purposes" (AT #2)
"Eliminating Barriers" (PC-7)
"Conquest of Illusion" (PC-8)
"Spiritual Implants" (PC-11)
"Games & Universes" (PC-12)
"Spiritual Machinery" (PC-14)

Full use of this manual may also require:
"Systemology Biofeedback" and
"Systemology Procedures"

<u>*Advanced Manuals should be studied in the*</u>
<u>*sequential order in which they are numbered.*</u>

First Edition Pocket Paperback — *February 2024*

mardukite.com

The Keys to the Kingdom
are Yours for the Taking!

The official Mardukite Systemology
"Advanced Training Course" is now
available in print for the first time.

Those Seekers that have completed the
"Pathway to Ascension" Systemology
Professional Course can now access the
upper-level teachings of our tradition.

This book is not for everyone...
This is the third manual for Level-7.

Never before has Joshua Free presented
this material outside the confines of the
Mardukite NexGen Systemology Society.

Learn how to expertly apply our
spiritual technology toward reaching
higher levels of Awareness and
Beingness than ever before thought
possible for humanity on planet Earth.

Each of the "Keys to the Kingdom"
Advanced Training Course Manuals
will further a Seekers reach on the
Pathway leading out of this Universe.

The Pathway to Ascension
Professional Course Lesson Booklet Series

#1 – *Increasing Awareness (Level-0)*
#2 – *Thought & Emotion (Level-0)*
#3 – *Clear Communication (Level-0)*
#4 – *Handling Humanity (Level-1)*
#5 – *Free Your Spirit (Level-2)*
#6 – *Escaping Spirit-Traps (Level-2)*
#7 – *Eliminating Barriers (Level-3)*
#8 – *Conquest of Illusion (Level-3)*
#9 – *Confronting the Past (Level-4)*
#10 – *Lifting the Veils (Level-4)*
#11 – *Spiritual Implants (Level-5)*
#12 – *Games and Universes (Level-5)*
#13 – *Spiritual Energy (Level-6)*
#14 – *Spiritual Machinery (Level-6)*
#15 – *The Arcs of Infinity (Level-6)*
#16 – *Alpha Thought (Level-6)*

Keys to the Kingdom
Advanced Training Course Manuals

#1 – *The Secret of Universes (Level-7)*
#2 – *Games, Goals & Purposes (Level-7)*
#3 – *The Jewel of Knowledge (Level-7)*
#4 – *Implanted Universes (Level-7)*
#5 – *Entities & Fragments (Level-8)*

Advanced Training Supplemental Booklets

#1 – *Systemology Biofeedback*
#2 – *Systemology Procedures*

TABLET OF CONTENTS

INTRODUCTION TO THE MANUAL

A.T. MANUAL #3:
THE JEWEL OF KNOWLEDGE

APPENDIX

"MANY YEARS AGO, I REALIZED
THAT 'THE WAY OUT' WOULD
SYSTEMATICALLY RESEMBLE
THE ROUTES BY WHICH WE
ORIGINALLY DESCENDED."
—*Joshua Free*
Backtrack Lectures, 2023

INTRODUCTION TO
THE MANUAL

This manual is restricted to students on
The Systemology Advanced Training Course
that have already completed the
"Pathway to Ascension" Professional Course

References to prerequisite material:
"The Secret of Universes" (AT #1)
"Games, Goals & Purposes" (AT #2)
"Eliminating Barriers" (PC-7)
"Conquest of Illusion" (PC-8)
"Spiritual Implants" (PC-11)
"Games & Universes" (PC-12)
"Spiritual Machinery" (PC-14)

Full use of this manual may also require:
"Systemology Biofeedback" and
"Systemology Procedures"

THE SYSTEMOLOGY
ADVANCED TRAINING COURSE
MANUAL SERIES

Mardukite Systemology is a new evolution in Human understanding about the "systems" governing *Life*, *Reality*, the *Universe* and all *Existences*. It is also a *Spiritual Path* used to transcend the Human experience and reach *"Ascension."*

This is an *Advanced Training* (*AT*) course manual detailing *upper-levels* of our spiritual philosophy. It is intended to assist *advancing* a *Seeker's* personal progress toward the *upper-most levels* of the *Pathway*.

This manual follows after our *Professional Course* series of lessons—available as individual booklets, or collected in two volumes titled *"The Pathway to Ascension"* The *Professional Course* follows after material given in the *Basic Course* booklets, or *"Fundamentals of Systemology"* volume.

11

The systematic methodology that we use to assist an individual to increase their *"Actualized Awareness"* (and reach gradually higher toward their *"Spiritual Ascension"*) is referred to as *"The Pathway"* — and that individual is called a *"Seeker."*

To receive the greatest benefit from this manual: it is expected that a *Seeker* will already be familiar with the fundamental concepts and terminology (previously relayed in the *Basic Course* and *Professional Course* lessons) of our *applied philosophy.*

As a *Seeker* increases their *Awareness* in this lifetime, their spiritual *"Knowingness"* also increases—which is to say their *certainty* on *Life*, on this and other *Universes*, and on *realizing Self* as an unlimited "spiritual being" *having* an enforced restrictive "human experience." A *Seeker* also *knowingly* increases their command and control of the "human experience." And this is a part of what is meant by *"Actualized Awareness."*

CHARTING FLIGHTS ON THE PATHWAY

Although there is a systematic structure to *fragmentation,* the personal journey experienced along the *Pathway* will be different for each *Seeker.* For example, certain areas will seem more *"turbulent"* or difficult for one *Seeker* than another. We tend to say that these areas have more *"charge"* on them—or that they are more *"heavily charged."* It is best to handle such areas when you are already feeling "good" and not in a situation (or condition) where that specific area is consistently being *"triggered"* or *"restimulated."*

As an applied philosophy, *Systemology* "theory" can be easily utilized in the "laboratory" of the "world-at-large" in everyday life. This is implied within the basic instruction of each lesson. Unlike other "sciences" that conduct experiments by making a change to some "objective variable" *out there* and waiting to see an effect, our focus is the individual (or *Observer*) themselves, and how *they* affect the "*Reality*" perceived.

Our philosophy is applied by using specific exercises and systematic techniques. These "*processes*" provide the most stable personal gain (and *realizations*) for each area; but only when actually applied with a *Seeker's* full "*presence*" and *Awareness*. Hundreds of such *processes* may be found in the "*Pathway to Ascension*" (*Professional Course*) material.

Applying a technique is called "*running a process.*" *Processes* are designed with very simple instructions or "*command-lines.*" To *run* a *processing command-line*, a *Seeker* may be assisted by the communication of that *line* from a "*Co-Pilot*" (as in "*Traditional Piloting*"). But even then, a *Seeker* must still personally "input" the *command* as *Self*. For this reason—and quite thankfully—*Solo-Processing* is possible.

TAKING FLIGHT ON THE PATHWAY

Processing Techniques are intended to treat the *Spiritual Being* or *Alpha-Spirit*; the individual themselves. The "*command-lines*" are *directed to* the individual themselves—not some *mental machinery* of theirs, and not even a *Biofeedback* metering device.

Systematic Processing is applied by the *Alpha-Spirit*—who then *Self-directs* command of their "Mind-System" or "body" (*genetic-vehicle*), both of which are "constructs" that the *Alpha-Spirit* (*Self*, or the "I-AM" *Awareness unit*) operates, but neither of which is actually *Self. Fragmentation* causes *Humans* to falsely identify *Self as* the "*Mind*" or even a "*Body.*"

Some *processes* can be treated quite lightly at first; others may require a bit of working at in order to get "*running*" well. It is important to set aside a period of time when you can be dedicated to your studies and *processing*. This period of time is referred to as a *"processing session."* When a *process* does start *running* well, it is important to be able to complete it to a satisfactory *"end-point."*

Processing allows us to be able to *actually* "look" at *things* and even determine the *considerations* we have made—or attitudes we have decided—about *Reality* as a result of those experiences.

It doesn't do us much good to simply "glance"—or to *restimulate* something uncomfortable and then quickly *withdraw* from it once again, leaving more of our *attention* yet again behind and held fixedly on it.

Generally speaking, a *Seeker* continues to *run* a *process* so long as something is "happening"—which is to say, the *process* is still producing a change. Usually this is evident by the type of "answers" that a *command-line* prompts a *Seeker* to originate from the database of their own *Mind-System*.

Processing Command-Lines ("PCL") are not "magic words"; they do not "do" anything on their own. They systematically assist a *Seeker* to direct their own attention toward increasing *Awareness*.

A *Seeker* may also cease to generate new "data" from a *process* without reaching an *"ultimate" realization* as an *"end-point."* It is possible that additional "layers" (or even other "areas") require handling before anything "deeper" is accessible. If this is the case, end the *process*. But, if a *Seeker* is *withdrawing* from something uncomfortable that was incited or stirred up, then a *process* is *run* until they feel "good" about it.

One of the benefits to *Flying-Solo* on the *Pathway* is that the *processing* is entirely *Self-determined*. This naturally provides a certain built-in "safety" for a practitioner. Anything you *restimulate* by *Self-determinism* is *your thing*. It is not triggered or incited by some external *"other-determined"* influences (or other "source-points") that make you an *effect*. It can be more easily handled in *processing*—or you can simply let things "cool down" and come back to it again in another *session*.

While it may seem "mysterious" to beginners, a *Seeker* gets a sense for knowing how long to *run* a *process* only with practice. Once you have spent some time actually applying material from *"The Pathway to Ascension"* Professional Course, there are many aspects of it that become "second nature" because they are, in fact, a part of our true original native nature. All we have done in *Systemology* is *"reverse engineer"* the routes of *creation* and *consideration* that are already *our own*.

Advanced Manuals should be studied in the sequential order in which they are numbered.

SYSTEMOLOGY LEVEL-7

We are publishing *"upper-level"* *Systemology* in 2024 for the very first time. Its application is dependent on a *Seeker* reaching a stable point of *"Beta-Defragmentation."* This requires proper use of materials for previous *processing-levels* — as given in the *"Pathway to Ascension"* *Professional Course*. Of course, we don't refer to such an individual as *"defragmented"* — which only further reinforces that *something* exists to *defragment* — but instead, as having reached a *Beta-state* of *Self-Honesty.* This "state" *must* be reached in order to go further.

Up to this point, a *Seeker* has become *"better-abled"* in the *game* of *"Being Human."* They have learned to play the *game* of *Beta-Existence* better — while still *on Earth,* and possibly still quite fixated on a

"*Human Body.*" Yet, the completion of *Systemology Level-6* is still a stable point of accomplishment—and well above the level of *Awareness* maintained by the "standard-issue" *Human Condition*. The individual is less likely to fall into as many *traps* and is more able to "brush off" most additional *fragmentation* before it accumulates.

"*Alpha-Defragmentation*" is what the "*Keys to the Kingdom*" *Advanced Training Course* manuals pertain to. Our aim is still for "*metahuman destinations.*" The goal of *Systemology Level-7* is to "safely" deliver (or *Pilot*) a *Seeker* to the *next plateau* "in sight" from the stable point already reached. There is, of course, something of a *chasm* between these points. So, it is necessary for a *Seeker* to be certain they have relieved themselves of enough "baggage" and "weight" (of *spiritual fragmentation*) in order to get enough "lift" for their ascent.

In the past, a few have even stumbled upon this point of *"crossing the abyss"* within their own traditions. But without *defragmentation*, their new-found vigor and horsepower causes them to just more quickly and deeply get lost in various distracting spiritual detours and intellectual tangents; or even fall back to old patterns, if they cannot maintain *Self-Honesty*.

This *chasm* is *not* a pitfall for *processing* mistakes—or even an *actual* barrier. But it is a "drop-off" point that many *perceive* upon reaching this part of their journey. It is sometimes enough to keep a *Seeker* from going further on the *Pathway*, fearing that they risk their existing gains. Therefore, we held off presenting the *upper-levels* until our presentation/communication of the *Pathway* had been perfected—and *Seekers* could approach this material with greater *certainty* and *ability-to-confront* its *reality*.

An *advanced Seeker* is likely to spend many months, and over *100 processing-hours*, on *Systemology Level-7*.

The *four* manuals—*"The Secret of Universes," "Games, Goals & Purposes," "The Jewel of Knowledge"* and *"Implanted Universes"*—should be treated as a single "unit" of uninterrupted work. This doesn't mean handling it as a single *session*—nor are all *Seekers* in a position to take a *retreat* from their *lives*. But daily *restimulation*, or other distractions, can significantly affect progress at this stage. Completing *Level-7* may require longer and more frequent *sessions* to achieve the same steady gains that one is previously used to.

Systemology Level-7 concerns primarily *"Games"*—which is also to say *"Universes."* On the *Standard Model*, *"Games and Universes"* is plotted at *"6.0"*—subordinate to the *"Alpha Thought"* (*"7.0"*) required to *postulate* or *create* the *"Game/*

Universe" into existence. This is senior to "*Intention*" at "5.0" — which is, of course, dependent upon some "*game-condition*" for any other *consideration* to occur. [This full description provides a perspective for just what "*upper-level*" part of the *Pathway* we are now treating with *Systemology Level-7*.]

Review these prerequisite materials first:
PC Lesson-7, "Eliminating Barriers"
PC Lesson-8, "Conquest of Illusion"
PC Lesson-11, "Spiritual Implants"
PC Lesson-12, "Games & Universes"
PC Lesson-14, "Spiritual Machinery"
AT Manual #1, "The Secret of Universes"
AT Manual #2, "Games, Goals & Purposes"

A.T. MANUAL #3
THE JEWEL OF
KNOWLEDGE

THE MIND-SYSTEM & "THE JEWEL"

The *Alpha-Spirit* carries a *fragmented Mind-System* with it from one *Beta-Existence* (any *Universe*) to another—and all the while they experience *existence*. This is the *real "baggage"* we are accumulating as a *Spiritual Beingness*. As a *Being*, we are simply a *point* or *unit* of *Awareness*, with no *mass* or *frequency*. But, the *Mind-System* (we *project* and *identify with* as part of that *Beingness*) *can* be affected by *Implants* and *mental-machinery*—and various *platforms* that provided a place for *layers-of-consideration* to accumulate as we progressed into *denser,* more *fixed* and *solid, existences.*

The *Mind-System* is *unknowingly* and *compulsively created* by the *Alpha-Spirit*. It is their *own* to handle. It is also their *own* primary stumbling-block to reaching *Asc-*

ension. It is the *fragmented* part of one's *Self* that has actually been opposing the individual all along. And of course, it is what we handled in bits and layers with previous *systematic processing-levels*. The *Pathway to Ascension* requires "freeing" an individual from the cumulative conditions that have been *created*, and continue to be, imposed on *Self*.

Previously on the *Pathway,* we have handled Beta-Defragmentation Procedures aimed at elevating *Actualized Awareness* to *above* "4" on the *Standard Model* (or *Zu-Line*). This is a point just beyond, or *"exterior to,"* a *fragmented Mind-System*. Of course, the *Mind-System* is still quite active—its *automated reactive-machinery* is still being *unknowingly created*. But a *Seeker* is regaining greater control of its activity. They are "freeing" their *point-of-view,* which is otherwise *compulsively* buried beneath it—or *entangled up* within it. *Higher-level processing* requires operating from a stable *viewpoint* that is *"exterior to"* the *Mind-System*.

A *fragmented Mind-System* (operating apart from, or outside, *Self-Honesty*) contains *fragmented purposes*—*Implanted considerations* and *goals*—that distort an *Alpha-Spirit's own actual goals* and *Self-determined purposes*. This is how our original *goal* *"To Create"* became inverted as *"To Survive."* A *fragmented individual* is more strongly the *effect of* the *Implanting* and *automated machinery*—*unknowingly*, and hence, *unwillingly*.

Considerations that we maintain with *conviction*—and as *Alpha-Thought*—are *"creations."* They have a certain degree of *fragmented energetic-mass* to them, which we often refer to as a *"charge."* Such a *"charge"* indicates that some part of our *Awareness* is still on them, keeping them *created* and held in a *suspended state* of *existence* as a *"rigid wave-form"* or *"solid ridge."*

This *A.T.* *"Keys to the Kingdom"* series of manuals explores upper-level *Alpha-Defragmentation*—or *The Way Out*. It requires fully clearing the *rigid-blocks* and *barriers* that are restricting an individual's *free access* to the *Beyond*; it requires being fully *at Cause* over the *Mind-System*. And in one form or another: this has always been the ultimate goal behind all *spiritualism*, *mysticism*, and the like. We have to *"clear the slate"* of *reality-agreements* for *this Universe* before one looks to treat anything beyond it. Failure to do so only results in *"dead-end religions"* that propose to know *"all about God"* (*"Infinity"*) in spite of having *no reality* on anything else.

Since there is a tremendous amount of content to cover in *this* manual: information that is contained in former lessons and manuals will not be repeated. It is a *Seeker's* responsibility to review that material.

The original *"Jewel of Knowledge"* is described in *AT Manual #1*. Elements of the original *"Jewel of Knowledge"* reappear in subsequent imitation *"False Jewels"* used for *"Entry-Point"* implanting-incidents into any *Beta-Existence* (*Universe*). These *"False Jewel"* Implants are never *constructed* to the same degree of complexity and beauty as the original *"Jewel of Knowledge"* experience that occurred prior to *"Home Universe."*

A full and direct handling of the Original *"Jewel of Knowledge"* would be purely speculative from this level of the *Pathway* (and while still *interior to this Physical Universe*). Besides: what we are *really* working toward on a much more *practical level* is *The Way Out* of *this Physical Universe*, and that requires handling the specific (and more accessible) *reality-agreements* that we are very much attached to *this Physical Universe*.

"The Jewel"—or more accurately, *"False Jewel"*—treated in *this manual* reflects that

specific *"construct"* which we *"passed through"* on *Entry-to-<u>this</u>-Universe* — meaning *this Physical Universe*. The complete *Implanting-Incident* that occurs upon *"Entry-into-this-Universe"* has two parts:

Part One: The False Jewel Implant
　　　　 Incident (Ref: *AT Manual #1*)

Part Two: The Heaven Implant Incident
　　　　 (Ref: *PC-12; AT Manual #1 & #2*)

"The Jewel" *Defragmentation Procedure* is not treated with techniques that a *Seeker* may be used to. It does not naturally *"process out"* using our standard *Beta-Defragmentation* practices. For example: properly *"confronting the past"* requires *Knowing* the proper *"timing"* and *"duration"* of an *event*. Such data is too distorted or *"falsely implanted"* for us to treat *"The Jewel"* with *Beta-Defragmentation* procedures. However, the time spent effectively handling earlier *processing-levels* will greatly reduce the amount of time an

advanced *Seeker* will require to properly complete *this* procedure.

Failure to complete basic *Beta-Defragmentation* (e.g. "*The Pathway to Ascension*" *Professional Course*) and have an understanding of previous *A.T. Manuals* and *supplements* will result in a *Seeker* easily becoming *overwhelmed* or *confused*—and therefore, struggling to achieve the results intended with this manual.

> Without the prerequisite background, *this* procedure could be *run infinitely* with no gains, or even negative results, potentially *invalidating* the *upper-level* progress a *Seeker* has thus far achieved. Additionally, a *Seeker* must *fully understand* and have *total certainty* on the procedural instructions given in the next section *before* applying—or even *reading*—*any* techniques from this manual.

In previous lessons (and manuals), we

have revealed how *"opposing considerations"* held with *equal conviction* (or *"charge"*)—such as *"there is something there"* and *"there is nothing there"*—are *Implanted*. Or, *get the idea* of being hypnotically-commanded to simultaneously *"go away!"* and *"stay where you are!"* This is the type of *confusion* and *uncertainty* that a *fragmented Mind-System* provides an individual. This is what maintains the *"solidity"* of *reality-agreements* for *this Physical Universe* by those experiencing it.

When combined with data for the *"Heaven Incident"* (in previous material), *"The Jewel" Procedure* unwraps the entire basic sequence of *considerations* (*postulates*) *Implanted* for the *Game* of *this Physical Universe*. [It undoubtedly also contains some common *Implant*-elements from the previous *Beta-Existence*, since that is where it was *constructed*.]

Implanting is most effective on us when it is part of a *"chain"* of reoccurring use. As we know from *AT Manual #1*: before being fully *entrapped*, a single visit to a *Prison-Penalty Universe* is seldom enough to "stick" an *Alpha-Spirit*. But, repeated reinforcement (*entry-incidents*) builds up a greater *energetic-mass* on whatever is being *Implanted.* Generally this coincides with our increased *protest* or *resistance* to it each time. If not handled properly by an advanced *Seeker*, "*The Jewel*" *Procedure* could theoretically *add* more "*mass*" rather than *defragment* what's there.

> "*The Jewel*" *Procedure* peels back a "layer" of *fragmentation* that is only exposed and accessible after fully completing *Systemology Levels 0-6* and the previous *AT Manuals*. *Systemology Level-7* is entirely *Solo-Piloted* (whether or not a *Seeker* was *Co-Piloted* formerly). To be handled with any certainty: the territory a *Solo-Pilot* must cover in *this Manual* really requires the assistance of a *Biofeedback Device* (*GSR-Meter*).

"The Jewel" Procedure is *not* a *"do-a-little-whenever-you-can"* type of activity that you *fit in* between daily *upsets* of normal *"Human"* living. Such means handling excessive *"preventative fundamentals"* (*flow-factor breaks, human problems, &tc.*) at the start of every *session—before* you can get on with resuming the actual procedure. Very little real progress is achieved that way; because this procedure will require *many sessions*.

For the duration of handling this procedure, a *Seeker* should place themselves in *conditions* (*environments*) that are suitable for *processing* this to its entirety, maintaining their own sense of *Self-Honest* stability throughout, and an ability to provide full *Awareness* to their *presence-in-session*. [This is not an appropriate period to embark on *"family vacations"* or take on greater *"material world"* responsibilities, &tc.]

This procedure is a *real test* of a *Seeker's* *Solo-Piloting* skills and level of *Awareness*.

It is a long and tedious *Intensive Procedure,* not an exercise in being entertained. The required level of interest maintained must be entirely *Self-determined* and *Self-directed.* Full completion of this *"step"* on the *Pathway* will provide the next stable *"landing zone"* (or *foundation*) from which to *Pilot* all additional *Alpha-Defragmentation.*

PROCEDURAL INSTRUCTIONS

This manual is a *"workbook"* of sorts; *not* an *"educational read-through"* book. It presents an *Intensive Procedure* without any perceptible *"gradients"* of progress along the way. It is handled as a single *unit* of work—the equivalent of an *entire processing-level*—and it requires many repetitive *steps* to complete..

A *Seeker* must have *total certainty* on these *instructions*—and all relevant background data from other lessons and manuals—before starting the actual procedure. New technical material is found in these instructions that a *Seeker* will need to review several times by itself, and then in relation to previous material, to fully understand.

An advanced *Seeker* should expect a minimum of *100 processing-hours* to complete this manual. This is best accomplished with *daily formal sessions* between *one* and *two hours*. [Preferably closer to *one hour*, the same time each day, as like a *"ritual."*]

THE IMPLANTING INCIDENT

Once the data for an *Implant-Platform "resurfaces"* with *systematic processing*, it must be handled (*processed-out*) fully, or else will remain in *restimulation* (even between *sessions*). This whole procedure is treating a single entire *Implanting-Incident*. A *Seeker's* attention will remain focussed on that *past incident* for the duration of this procedure until its completion.

We are treating the earliest, most basic, and significant *Implanting-Incident* connected to our experience of *this Physical Universe.* The *Implant* was masterfully *constructed*—specifically designed to remain *hidden* and *non-confronted.* It is not meant to be easily *recalled* or "*spotted*" on the *Backtrack*—and it requires a precise *systematic procedure* in which to *knowingly* "*contact*" it with our *Awareness* and *defragment* its content.

There is the possibility of being "*ejected*" from the *Incident* during *processing.* We mean that while *attention* is on it, something occurs to redirect our *attention* elsewhere—usually on some activity of the *Mind-System.* If the *Incident* suddenly "disappears," becomes "inaccessible," or seems "unreal," during the procedure, then the *Seeker* has likely been "*ejected.*" We aren't erasing "memory" of the *Incid-*

ent; we are *defragmenting* the portion of our *Mind-System* that is *unknowingly* and *fixedly* maintaining *considerations* from the *Incident*. A *Seeker* simply redirects attention to "*return*" to the *exact point* of the procedure that they were *ejected from*.

As with other *incident-running processes*, a *Seeker* should be familiar with the practice of "*returning to (such and such) a time*" with their *Awareness*. This is done by *intention* and must be *Self-directed* by a *Solo-Pilot*. This procedure is really one exceptionally long *process*. A *Seeker* may also be ending a *session* at some arbitrary point within it—such as: *Cycle-D; Part 3, Step-19*. To start up again, or if *ejected*, a *Seeker* must reorient their *Awareness* in the *Incident* at the exact point they left off. Therefore, the appropriate "*Cycle/Part/Step*" data is inserted in the *first* procedural PCL of the *next session*:

"*Return to ___ of the Basic Implant-Incident.*"

But what do we mean by *Cycles*, *Parts* and *Steps*? To *process-out* this *Incident*, a *Seeker* must *run* the entire *Incident*— which is an entire "*series*" of *Implants*. Since we have *systematic* data for the complete *pattern* of this *series*, we do not need to "*trace*" any "*chains*" back to *earlier incidents* (such as with other types of *fragmentation*). This procedure *starts* with the literal *beginning* of the *Incident* and *runs* through its entirety.

"*The Jewel*" *Procedure* mimics the full *series-pattern* of this particular *Implanting-Incident*. It consists of only *five* different *Parts* (each with many *Steps*). But, those same *five Parts* are repeated *ten times* for the duration of the *Incident*. A *Seeker* essentially *runs* all *ten Cycles* of the *five Parts*. This means that the complete procedure consists of *50 total parts* to *process*.

To be clear: *Parts 1, 2, 3, 4,* and *5,* are repeated in that order, *ten times*. Or, to rephrase: each *Cycle* consists of *Parts 1, 2, 3,*

4, and 5; and there are *ten Cycles* total. To avoid confusion, we label *each* of the *Cycles* with a *letter "A"* through *"J."* This means that in *Cycle-A*, a *Seeker runs Parts 1, 2, 3, 4,* and 5; then proceeds to *Cycle-B, running Parts 1, 2, 3, 4,* and 5; and so on, through *Cycle-J.* Another way of stating this: a *Seeker runs A1, A2, A3, A4, A5*; then *B1, B2, B3, B4, B5*... Why is this so important to keep track of?

The only way to really get *"stuck"* in this procedure is either *skipping Steps,* or treating a *Cycle* out of sequence. The *Incident* was meant to be *confusing*; and for an *Alpha-Spirit* to lose track of their place within it. Even though *Part 1,* for example, is always *run* like *Part 1.* The *Part 1* of *Cycle-A* is not the same point in the *Incident* as *Part 1* of *Cycle-D, &tc.*

Do not make marks within this manual. A *Seeker* is prompted to make their own "worksheets." The first *"worksheet"* a *Seeker* should prepare for themselves is a "table" or "chart" whereby they can "check off" the *Parts* of each *Cycle* as they are completed. The following "table" gives an example, with "x" marks to indicate each of the *50 total parts* that compose the entire *Incident.*

CHECKSHEET		PARTS				
		1	**2**	**3**	**4**	**5**
CYCLE	**A**	x	x	x	x	x
	B	x	x	x	x	x
	C	x	x	x	x	x
	D	x	x	x	x	x
	E	x	x	x	x	x
	F	x	x	x	x	x
	G	x	x	x	x	x
	H	x	x	x	x	x
	I	x	x	x	x	x
	J	x	x	x	x	x

Parts 1, 2, and *3,* mostly consist of straightforward *"command-item"* lines. They have a significance that is understood with *language*—and therefore are *processed* "verbally" (spoken). Of course, the original *Implant* does not include

"English" words; but we approximate their associated meaning in *systematic processing.* [Refer to *PC Lessons 11* and *12.*]

Parts 4 and *5,* consist of a precise *pattern* of *"object-items"* that have *no verbal-language* component. These *"item lines"* are run *silently.* The PCL used simply directs *Awareness* to perceive *"object-items"* in specific ways—in mimicry of how they appeared in the actual *Incident.*

STANDARD PROCEDURE

Traditional Piloting of *"The Jewel" Procedure* is *Solo* with a *GSR-Meter.* If the *Biofeedback Device* normally uses *two-handed electrodes*, they are combined or coupled for *one-hand* use, but still kept separate to avoid directly touching each other and short-circuiting. The *Meter electrode-sensor* is held in the non-writing hand, leaving the other hand free to flip-over *"worksheets"* after making *marks* on them.

To make *processing* and handling *work-sheets* easier, they should be on single pieces of loose paper; not a notebook or journal—using paperclips if necessary; never staples. They should be kept organized and safe between *sessions*. This manual is prepared in many formats; its current size and binding will determine if it is appropriate to use during *processing*.

In most cases, a *Seeker* will title a *work-sheet* at the top, with the *"Cycle,"* and *"Part,"* then simply list the "item line" numbers (or *Steps*) for that *Part* as a column down the left-hand side of the sheet (or multiple sheets) to keep track of the *"Meter-reads"* and the completed progress.

Materials need to be handled in *session* in such a way that they do not unnecessarily disturb the motions of the hand holding the *GSR-electrode-sensor*. The *worksheets* are best handled as stacks. The ones with the listed "item line" numbers that you intend to mark on should be closest to your writing hand. The complete ones can be flipped over face down and set as a stack further away on the table.

If pages of this edition of the manual are difficult to keep open easily for processing, then a *Seeker* may need to prepare a second stack of *worksheets* that are essentially complete copies of the "*Implant Platform*" sections, listing out all the actual "*Implant Item*" lines from this manual. Whether you use a book or separate *Implant-Item worksheets*, it is common practice to cover the upcoming "*item lines*" with a notecard or additional sheet of paper that may be moved down to expose the next "*item*" to view only when the *Seeker* is ready for it.

The most basic *worksheets* are simply "*numbered*" to match the "*items*" listed for an *Implant-Platform*. Any *worksheets* intended for use must be prepared sequentially and arranged prior to the *session*. It is also important to avert the *Body's Eyes* when they are being changed (flipped-over into a *"done"* pile) so that *attention* does not fall on a new *"worksheet"* (or *"item"* list) before it is ready to be properly handled.

This procedure is not *run* like other *processes.* In other types of *processing,* one might use a *Biofeedback Device* to identify areas with the *"most fragmented charge"* — such as from a list of possible *terminals, &tc.* In this current procedure: we already know that there *is* a *"charge"* of some degree on *each* one of the *"implant items."* The current goal is to *"contact"* that *"charge"* and *defragment ("discharge") it* — and the *Biofeedback Device* is often quite necessary for a *Seeker* to know when these conditions (*contact* and *defragmentation*) occur—between when a *Meter* *"reads"* or *"registers"* (*a change in state*) and when it no longer *"reads"* for an *"item."*

For this procedure: (unlike in previous *processing-levels*) we do not want to allow for a lot of *"mental activity"* — *"freewheeling thought"* or even *considerations* — that is not specifically directed on *"spotting"* the *command-item*. While *processing* the various *Parts* and *Cycles* of the *Incident*, additional *"sensory data"* (about the *Incident*) *may resurface*, and if it does, it should be noted on your *worksheet* before continuing the *process*. It is *not* actually advisable to intentionally go *looking for* this data during *defragmentation*.

STANDARD DEFRAGMENTATION
(WITH A GSR-METER)

The basic instructions for this procedure are to repeatedly *"spot with attention"* (and thereby *confront*) each *"implant-item"* (a *"command-item"*-type *postulate* or *"object-item"*) listed for an *Implant-Platform* until it has no further *"charge"* — meaning that it no longer *"reads"* (or *registers*) on a

GSR-Meter. This form of *defragmentation* is possible only due to the increased level of *Awareness* available to a *Seeker* by this point on the *Pathway.*

However, a *Seeker* should not *"decide"* (*postulate*) anything *in-session* during the procedure. At this level of development, a *Seeker's "Alpha-Thought"* is actualized enough that it is possible for them to *"decide"* that something is now *"defragmented"* and then cause it to cease *registering* on the *Meter.* But this likely will leave a *suppressed charge* remaining on that *"item"* — and that only complicates continuing the procedure from there.

For example: a *Seeker* can get "bored" with the procedure and *decide* that an item will no longer *register* — and it *will.* It is also important not to make any *decisions* about how many times an *"item" should read* on a *Meter* based on how many times a previous *"item"* (*&tc.*) had *registered.*

An *"item"* may *Meter-read* only *once* or it may *register* twenty times. Since an *"item"* *may* only *register* once, the *Device*, manuals and worksheets should be arranged so a *Seeker* is able to "catch" *all reads* as they occur. The exact number of times necessary to *spot* (and *defragment*) is not the same for all *items* or all *individuals*. [This makes *Solo-Piloting* this procedure *without* a *GSR-Meter* quite challenging.]

As a *Seeker* is familiar with from *PC Lesson-11*, *&tc.*, an *Implant-Platform* is not *defragmented* simply by an individual reading or skimming over its printed content. Each of these *"items"* needs to be *"contacted with attention"* *in-session*, in such a way that it *does* produce a *"Meter-read."* The *Seeker* "runs" an *"item"* (a numbered *processing line*), until it produces no *"Meter-reads"* *three times in a row.* Only then does the cover-sheet get moved down to reveal and handle the next *"item"* in the list.

THE "LIGHT" & THE "ALPHA-SPIRIT"

There are two *new* elements of *processing* that we must introduce for this procedure. As we have said (above): each one of the *"items"* has a *"charge"* on it that *registers* on a *Meter* when it is initially *"contacted"* in-session with our *Awareness*. And then it proceeds to *"Meter-read"* until it is *"discharged."* But how does a *Seeker* ensure they are properly directing an *intention* to *"contact"* the *"item"* and get the first *"read"*?

The actual *charge* on each *Implanted-Item* is connected to an *"impression"* (or *"perception,"* if you prefer) of the *Alpha-Spirit (Self)* at the exact moment each *item* was *Implanted.* This would be similar to seeing your *Body* from an *external* view while *running* an *incident* from a *Beta-Existence* experience. But this usually involves more "familiar" surroundings and *sensory facets* than an *"Entry-into-Universe"* or *"False Jewel"* experience.

At the time of the *Implanting-Incident*, you did not have an identifiable "*Body*" like you do now. There is also no "spatial-orientation" in the way you would describe experiences *within this Physical Universe.* So, the correct *systematic* PCL for this is: "*Spot the Alpha*" (meaning "*Alpha-Spirit*" —or one's own *Beingness*—at the moment of the *Implanted-Item*). This is done strictly by *intention*, although a *Seeker* may have to "feel around" a bit with their selectively directed *attention* before they get a "*Meter-read*" on "*contact.*"

The PCL "*Spot the Alpha*" is part of orienting *Awareness* during the *defragmentation* procedure; it is not a "*command-item*" from the actual *incident*. There is also the second *new* element for us to introduce, which is similar to, and usually combined with the action of "*Spotting the Alpha.*" *The Jewel Incident* included a special kind of "*Light*" that induces a "trance-like hypnotic groggy" receptive state in the *Alpha*

Spirit while an *"item"* is *Implanted*. In this wise, the PCL is: *"Spot the Light."* And this is also done strictly by *intention*—meaning selectively directing *attention*.

While *running* the *processes*, it is *not* necessary to actually *"see"* the *"Light"* or *"Alpha-Spirit"* (in *ZU-Vision* or as a literal *visualization*) in order to *"spot"* it with *Awareness* and get a *"Meter-read."* Also: one performs the procedure with the *eyes open*—using the *"Platform"* list, while still noting any *Biofeedback* responses. It is usually sufficient to simply be *aware* of what is taking place in the *incident* for a *Meter-read*.

As a matter of perspective: the *Light* comes from the distance, just off to the *"left side"* of directly in front of you. When *running* the *process*, when you *get the sense* (or *concept*) of what should be where it is, and *contact* it, this produces a *Meter-read*.

Although *Implanted "command-items" may* be "called out loud" for *defragmentation processing,* we seldom audibly verbalize other parts of a PCL—such as *"Spot the Light"* and *"Spot the Alpha"* —or else they are *"said" internally* to focus or direct *attention.*

The most common *processing command* (PCL) for this procedure uses the formula:

"Spot the {implanted-item}; Spot the Alpha."

However, in most cases, *"Spot the Alpha"* is also meant to include *"Spot the Light"* simultaneously as a combined single-action. A PCL is not as effective by adding a third component, so once we are handling an *implant-item* for the first part of a PCL, then the simultaneous *"Spot the Light; Spot the Alpha"* are simply combined for *systematic* purposes as *"Spot the Alpha."* [This "skill" in *spotting* the *Light* and the *Alpha-Spirit* are best practiced as part of the first *sessions* of this procedure; not separately, *out-of-session*.]

The pattern of some *Implant-Platforms* may require you to *spot/contact* one *item-phrase*, then a second *item-phrase*, and the finally both together as a single action. An example of this *pattern* would be:

Item-1: "To Be *A*."
Item-2: "To Be *B*."
Item-3: "To Be *A*; To Be *B*."

To be even more technically accurate, the full *pattern* in many cases is:

Item-1: *"To Be A; & Spot the Alpha."*
Item-2: *"To Be B; & Spot the Alpha."*
Item-3: *"To Be A, To Be B; & Spot the Alpha."*

The "proper way" for a *Seeker* to "contact," "visualize," or "get the sense" of connecting with a specific point of the incident—the "command-item"; "Light-Alp-

ha" combination, *&tc.*—is whatever produces the best *Meter-reads* on contact. Whatever an *Seeker* "does" to get *that Meter-read*, they continue doing it while "*spotting*" the "*item-line*" until it no longer *registers* for *three times* on *spotting* it.

Prior to applying this procedure, it would be worthwhile for a *Seeker* to practice "*seeing something*" with the same level of *interest* and *attention* as if "*for the first time.*" This is especially important where content from an *Implant-Platform* is partially viewed before its use in the actual procedure.

HANDLING THE PROCEDURE

Worksheets are prepared to keep track of the *Meter-reads* for each individual "*item*" in the procedure. This will mean making *ten* duplicate *worksheets* for each *Part*; one for each of the *ten Cycles*. The following is *only an example.* We will use a facsimile of the top of the same *"A1" worksheet* shown twice below to better illustrate handling the procedure as one progresses through it.

In this example: the first *item (1.0)* "*read*" four times, each marked with a "/" (*slash*), then gave "*no-read*" three times. These three "*no-reads*" at the end don't need to be marked, since it is a necessary condition for moving to the next *item*. The second *item (1.1.1)* "*read*" twice, each marked with a "/" (*slash*), followed by three "no-reads." The third *item (1.1.2)* "*read*" three times, then three "*no-reads.*" However, for whatever reason, the next *item* here *(1.1.3)* doesn't "*read*" at all three times from the start. So, what does a *Seeker* do?

```
CYCLE:A   PART:1   DATE:##/##/##
   1.0  ////
  1.1.1  //
  1.1.2  ///
  1.1.3  x
```

If *items* cease *discharging* easily (seeming more *solid* rather than *defragmenting*), or a new *item* does not give any *"reads"* three times right from the start, there may be *charge* still left on a recent prior *item*.

In this example: the *Seeker* puts an "x" in the space next to *1.1.3*. Since they are still near the top of the *Implant-Platform*, they decide to check the last few *item-lines* starting from the top. This implies another systematic use of the word *"backtrack."* Usually, a *Seeker* only *backtracks* one or two *items*. In this one area: experience with the procedure *may* aid getting a sense of how far one needs to *backtrack* when this occurs.

The *Seeker backtracks* to *1.0* and finds it still gives three *"no-reads"*; and they place an "x" there now. The same occurs for *1.1.1*; another "x." However, *1.1.2* is found to still have *charge* on it, and its *"newer reads"* are marked with a "\" (*backslash*) this time, to show that you have *backtracked* for those "*reads.*" In our example: it "*read*" four times before three "*no-reads.*" Now, *1.1.3* "*reads*" nine times before its three "*no-reads*"; and the *Seeker* continues with handling the *next item* in the *listed-sequence,* and so on until the end of that "*Platform.*"

```
CYCLE:A   PART:1   DATE:##/##/##
   1.0  //// x
   1.1.1  // x
   1.1.2  /// \\\\
   1.1.3  x /////////
```

Backtracking should be done sparingly and not as a solution to inexperience/improperly *contacting* a *listed item.* A *Seeker* must be careful to properly *direct attention* to the *backtracked item* just prior, and not accidentally put *attention* on the same *item* where it also appears earlier or later in the *Incident.* If a particular *item* just seems to keep *registering* on a *Meter* numerous times: be certain not to "*suppress*" it; keep *running* it until it fully *discharges.*

It is important to note, when handling this procedure: any extreme unpleasantness, pain, or sudden illness, is typically a result of *passing-over* or *suppressing* the *"charge"* from earlier *items;* or the mistaken redirection of *attention* on the same *item* in a later *Cycle* that has not yet been handled.

Most troubles with this procedure can be avoided by: understanding the *instructions;* understanding the meaning of any *words* used in a PCL or *"command-lines"*; seeing and recording all *Meter-reads;* making sure each *item* is fully *discharged* before continuing; not skipping any *Steps, Parts,* or *Cycles;* and finally, sticking with the procedure to its conclusion—and not getting distracted by "exploring" the *Mind-System* during these *sessions.*

Misunderstood words can affect *"reads."* And while the procedure has been found effective in its standard form, there are suggested alternative variations for some *words* used to represent certain *items*. Although the *Implanting-Incident* is uniform to *Entry-into-this-Universe*, we do allow for varying the standard form with these semantic variations—assuming an individual's interpretation of some parts of their experience differed slightly. The alternatives only appear for certain *items*; and are only used in cases where a *Seeker* is having difficulty getting a *"command-line"* to *"read"* in its standard wording.

HANDLING "PART-4" AND "PART-5"

Implanted-Items for *Part-4* and *Part-5* are *"object-items"* rather than *"command-items."* They are still *run* as PCL, but they involve perceiving various *shapes* and *constructs*. In this wise, it is important for a *Seeker* to understand the distinction between a *"transparent form"* (or *"outline"*) and a *"solid form"* of the same *shape*; and between a *"two-dimensional"* (2D) *square* or *circle*, and a *"three-dimensional"* (3D) *cube* or *sphere*, &tc.

Another critical clarification a *Seeker* should know for these *Parts*: the distinction between a *"tetrahedron"* (with *four*-sides/faces/facets, all *triangles*, including the *base*) and a *"pyramid"* (with *five*-sides total, four *triangle* faces/facets, and a *square* base).

For the purpose of *spotting* in the *incident*: the *"object-items"* all *appear* approximately three feet (or one meter) away from your *point-of-view* at *"head/eye-level."* There will be *one, two, three,* or *four* *"objects"* for each *item-line*. The position(s) of the *"object-item(s)"* for *processing* is based on the number/quantity of them.

1 *"object-item"*   : in-front
2 *"object-items"* : left-side + right-side
3 *"object-items"* : in-front, left-side + right-side
4 *"object-items"* : in-front, left-side + right-side, behind

```
    &           & = THE LIGHT
    X           X = OBJECT
 X  A  X            POSITIONS
    X           A = ALPHA-SPIRIT
```

When first *running* the procedure, practice *perceiving* the proper quantity of *object(s)* indicated on the *item-line* (PCL) as a single *intention*/action. The *object(s)* will either be *"going in / towards"* or *"going away"* (as indicated in the PCL). Such instructions for the *"motion"* are used for the *defragmentation* procedure and are not *"implanted messages"* from the *incident* itself. It *mimics* the sense of *motion* that was experienced in the *incident*. *"Spotting"* and *"contacting"* the *mass* of the *object(s)* is what produces the necessary *"Meter-reads."*

PROCEDURE COMPLETION

Upon completion of *"J5"*—the *tenth* and final *Cycle* of handling *Part-5*—a *Seeker* should have achieved a perceivable *"gain"* or a greatly increased sense of *"release/re-lief,"* &tc. If this is not the case—and the *fragmentation* actually seems more *"solid"* rather than *"erased"*—it is possible that another complete *series* of all ten *Cycles* of the same *Jewel Procedure* may need to be repeated using new *worksheets*.

Alternatively, there is also the possibility —due to the amount of time spent on the procedure, various separate *sessions*, and numerous repetitive *items*—that some *attention* may have "locked up" (become *entangled*) with some point of the actual *processing* (rather than the *charge* left on the *incident* itself). This basically means that *charge* was *added* to an *item-line* in the *present* during the *processing*.

If this appears to be the case: the *processing sessions* themselves can be "scanned" for *"locked up attention"* (using the *item-lists* and *Meter*). This type of "scanning" and *assessing* for *"within the last {number of} months, has any charge been left on {item}?"* only applies to repairing a *session-charge*; this does not work for *processing-out* the actual *Implanting-Incident*; it does not substitute the procedure. Hence, this should only be done *after* a full *series* of *ten Cycles* is completed

Because you are "scanning" an "*item*" for the entire duration you have been *running* the procedure, you only need to treat each "*list-item*" once. The *assessment-PCL* (given above) is for that "*list-item*" any time it appeared in the procedure (during that duration of time). If you get a "*read*" on something, you'd mark it on the sheet, then use the *Meter* to *assess* for which Cycle, *&tc.* Usually *spotting* that a *charge being added* has occurred (and knowing precisely *when* in the *session* and *where* in the *Platform-list* it occurred) is enough to resolve it with *Actualized attention/Awareness.*

The goal of this procedure is to actually "*erase*" or "*disperse*" the *mental-charge* that is maintained from this *incident*; *not* simply take *some of the weight off,* as we commonly find with other *processes.* This means handling even the most *subtle fragmentation* to an end-point; not only those aspects that seem the most obviously turbulent. There is also a critical difference in *spotting* a certain *Part/Step* in one *Cycle* (or time within the *incident*) from another.

This all being said: it has *not* yet been determined if an appropriately skilled *advanced Seeker* would actually be able to properly handle this procedure completely *without* the assistance of an appropriate *Biofeedback Device.* While there are other *processes* for *Systemology Level-7* and *Level-8*, where a *Seeker* might more easily get away with not using a *Meter*: we cannot, at this time, guarantee that for *this* specific part of the *Pathway.*

JEWEL PROCEDURE—PART 1

[Speak the "command-item" a few times out loud, and "spot the Alpha" (and "Light"); then speak the "command-item" while "spotting the Alpha" (and "Light"). Perform this in whatever way produces the best "Meter-reads."]

1.1.0 *Spot the Light; Spot the Alpha*

1.1.1 **TO BE NOBODY;**
& Spot the Alpha

1.1.2 **TO BE EVERYBODY;**
& Spot the Alpha

1.1.3 **TO BE NOBODY, TO BE EVERYBODY;**
& Spot the Alpha

1.2.1 **TO BE ME;** *& Spot the Alpha*

1.2.2 **TO BE YOU;** *& Spot the Alpha*

1.2.3 **TO BE ME, TO BE YOU;**
& Spot the Alpha

1.3.1 **TO BE MYSELF;**
    & Spot the Alpha
1.3.2 **TO BE OTHERS;**
    & Spot the Alpha
1.3.3 **TO BE MYSELF, TO BE**
    OTHERS; *& Spot the Alpha*

*possible alternate below *if 1.4.1* doesn't register, even with backtracking

1.4.1 **TO BE AN ANIMAL;**
    & Spot the Alpha
1.4.2 **TO BE ANIMALS;**
    & Spot the Alpha
1.4.3 **TO BE AN ANIMAL, TO BE**
    ANIMALS; *& Spot the Alpha*

if "...AN ANIMAL" won't read, try "TO BE A FISH."

1.5.0 *Spot the Light; Spot the Alpha*

1.5.1 **TO BE A BODY;**
    & Spot the Alpha
1.5.2 **TO BE BODIES;**
    & Spot the Alpha
1.5.3 **TO BE A BODY, TO BE**
    BODIES; *& Spot the Alpha*

1.6.1 **TO BE MATTER;**
 & Spot the Alpha

1.6.2 **TO BE SPACE;** *& Spot the Alpha*

1.6.3 **TO BE MATTER, TO BE SPACE;** *& Spot the Alpha*

1.7.1 **TO BE A SPIRIT;**
 & Spot the Alpha

1.7.2 **TO BE SPIRITS;**
 & Spot the Alpha

1.7.3 **TO BE A SPIRIT, TO BE SPIRITS;** *& Spot the Alpha*

*possible alternate below *if 1.8.1* doesn't register, even with backtracking

1.8.1 **TO BE A GOD;** *& Spot the Alpha*

1.8.2 **TO BE GODS;** *& Spot the Alpha*

1.8.3 **TO BE A GOD, TO BE GODS;**
 & Spot the Alpha

if "...A GOD" won't read, try "TO BE A METAHUMAN."

1.9.0 *Spot the Light; Spot the Alpha*

1.9.1 **TO DO NOTHING;**
 & Spot the Alpha

1.9.2 **TO DO EVERYTHING;**
& Spot the Alpha
1.9.3 **TO DO NOTHING, TO DO EVERYTHING;** *& Spot the Alpha*

1.10.1 **TO DO MUCH;** *& Spot the Alpha*
1.10.2 **TO DO LITTLE;**
& Spot the Alpha
1.10.3 **TO DO MUCH, TO DO LITTLE;**
& Spot the Alpha

*possible alternate below *if 1.11.2* doesn't register, even with backtracking

1.11.1 **TO DO IT ALL;** *& Spot the Alpha*
1.11.2 **TO DO NOT ANY;**
& Spot the Alpha
1.11.3 **TO DO IT ALL, TO DO NOT ANY;** *& Spot the Alpha*
*if "...NOT ANY" won't read, try "TO DO NOT ANYTHING."

1.12.1 **TO DO AMBITIOUSLY;**
& Spot the Alpha
1.12.2 **TO DO SLIGHTLY;**
& Spot the Alpha

70

1.12.3 **TO DO AMBITIOUSLY, TO DO SLIGHTLY;** *& Spot the Alpha*

1.13.0 *Spot the Light; Spot the Alpha*

1.13.1 **TO DO MORE;** *& Spot the Alpha*
1.13.2 **TO DO LESS;** *& Spot the Alpha*
1.13.3 **TO DO MORE, TO DO LESS;** *& Spot the Alpha*

1.14.1 **TO DO SPLENDIDLY;** *& Spot the Alpha*
1.14.2 **TO DO AWFULLY;** *& Spot the Alpha*
1.14.3 **TO DO SPLENDIDLY, TO DO AWFULLY;** *& Spot the Alpha*

1.15.1 **TO DO WISELY;** *& Spot the Alpha*
1.15.2 **TO DO FOOLISHLY;** *& Spot the Alpha*
1.15.3 **TO DO WISELY, TO DO FOOLISHLY;** *& Spot the Alpha*

1.16.1 **TO DO RIGHT;** *& Spot the Alpha*
1.16.2 **TO DO WRONG;** *& Spot the Alpha*

1.20.2 **TO HAVE POORLY;**
    & Spot the Alpha

1.20.3 **TO HAVE HUGELY, TO HAVE POORLY;** *& Spot the Alpha*

1.21.0 *Spot the Light; Spot the Alpha*

1.21.1 **TO HAVE GREEDILY;**
    & Spot the Alpha

1.21.2 **TO HAVE SELECTIVELY;**
    & Spot the Alpha

1.21.3 **TO HAVE GREEDILY, TO HAVE SELECTIVELY;**
    & Spot the Alpha

1.22.1 **TO HAVE MIGHTILY;**
    & Spot the Alpha

1.22.2 **TO HAVE SPARSELY;**
    & Spot the Alpha

1.22.3 **TO HAVE MIGHTILY, TO HAVE SPARSELY;** *& Spot the Alpha*

  *possible alternate below *if* 1.23.2 doesn't register, even with backtracking

1.23.1 **TO HAVE MAGNIFICENTLY;**
    & Spot the Alpha

1.23.2 **TO HAVE TAWDRILY;**
  & Spot the Alpha
1.23.3 **TO HAVE MAGNIFICENTLY,**
  TO HAVE TAWDRILY;
  & Spot the Alpha
 *if "...TAWDRILY" won't read, try "TO HAVE TASTELESSLY."

1.24.1 **TO HAVE TOTALITY;**
  & Spot the Alpha
1.24.2 **TO HAVE NEGATIVENESS;**
  & Spot the Alpha
1.24.3 **TO HAVE TOTALITY, TO HAVE NEGATIVENESS;**
  & Spot the Alpha

1.25.0 *Spot the Light; Spot the Alpha*

1.25.1 **TO STAY EVERYWHERE;**
  & Spot the Alpha
1.25.2 **TO STAY NOWHERE;**
  & Spot the Alpha
1.25.3 **TO STAY EVERYWHERE, TO STAY NOWHERE;**
  & Spot the Alpha

1.26.1 **TO STAY HERE;**
& Spot the Alpha
1.26.2 **TO STAY THERE;**
& Spot the Alpha
1.26.3 **TO STAY HERE, TO STAY THERE;** *& Spot the Alpha*

1.27.1 **TO STAY NEAR;**
& Spot the Alpha
1.27.2 **TO STAY FAR;** *& Spot the Alpha*
1.27.3 **TO STAY NEAR, TO STAY FAR;**
& Spot the Alpha

1.28.1 **TO STAY UP;** *& Spot the Alpha*
1.28.2 **TO STAY DOWN;**
& Spot the Alpha
1.28.3 **TO STAY UP, TO STAY DOWN;**
& Spot the Alpha

1.29.0 *Spot the Light; Spot the Alpha*

*possible alternate below *if Step-1.29.3* doesn't register, even with backtracking

1.29.1 **TO STAY OUT;** *& Spot the Alpha*
1.29.2 **TO STAY IN;** *& Spot the Alpha*

1.29.3 **TO STAY OUT, TO STAY IN;**
      & Spot the Alpha
    if "...OUT...IN" won't read, try reversing order of "OUT" and "IN."

1.30.1 **TO STAY BACK;**
      & Spot the Alpha
1.30.2 **TO STAY FORWARD;**
      & Spot the Alpha
1.30.3 **TO STAY BACK, TO STAY FORWARD;** *& Spot the Alpha*

1.31.1 **TO STAY EARLIER;**
      & Spot the Alpha
1.31.2 **TO STAY LATER;**
      & Spot the Alpha
1.31.3 **TO STAY EARLIER, TO STAY LATER;** *& Spot the Alpha*

    possible alternate below if 1.32.2 doesn't register, even with backtracking

1.32.1 **TO STAY PRESENT;**
      & Spot the Alpha
1.32.2 **TO STAY ABSENT;**
      & Spot the Alpha

1.32.3 TO STAY PRESENT, TO STAY
ABSENT; *& Spot the Alpha*

*if "...ABSENT" won't read, try "TO STAY AWAY."

JEWEL PROCEDURE—PART 2

[*Speak the "command-item" a few times out loud, and "spot the Alpha" (and "Light"); then speak the "command-item" while "spotting the Alpha" (and "Light"). Perform this in whatever way produces the best Meter-reads. Keep saying the "command-item" phrase as a "noun" or "terminal" while spotting the Alpha; performing this action until it no longer registers a read. Mark reads with a "/" (slash). If the next item-line doesn't register, check earlier line(s) and mark any backtracked reads with a "\" (backslash). Part-2 also takes excessive charge off of keywords used in Part-3.*]

  2.0 *Spot the Light; Spot the Alpha*

2.1 **THE NOW;** *& Spot the Alpha*

2.2 **THE PAST;** *& Spot the Alpha*

2.3 **THE FUTURE;** *& Spot the Alpha*

2.4 **THE TIME;** *& Spot the Alpha*

2.5 **THE SPACE;** *& Spot the Alpha*

2.6 **THE MOTION;** *& Spot the Alpha*

2.7 **THE ENERGY;** *& Spot the Alpha*

2.8 **THE MASSES;** *& Spot the Alpha*

2.9 **THE SELF;** *& Spot the Alpha*

2.10 **THE OTHERS;** *& Spot the Alpha*

2.11 **THE LIFE;** *& Spot the Alpha*

2.0 *Spot the Light; Spot the Alpha*

2.12 **THE EXISTENCE;**
& Spot the Alpha

2.13 **THE CONDITIONS;**
& Spot the Alpha

2.14 **THE EFFECTS;** *& Spot the Alpha*

2.15 **THE PICTURES;**
& Spot the Alpha

2.16 **THE MIND;** *& Spot the Alpha*

JEWEL PROCEDURE—PART 3

[Speak the "command-item" phrase a few times out loud, and "spot the Alpha" (and "Light"); speak the "command-item" while "spotting the Alpha" (and "Light"). Perform this in whichever way produces the best "reads" until that action no longer registers.]

3.21.1 **CREATING TO DESTROY THE UNIVERSE;** *& Spot the Alpha*

3.21.2 **DESTROYING TO CREATE THE UNIVERSE;**
& Spot the Alpha

3.21.3 **CREATING TO DESTROY THE UNIVERSE, DESTROYING TO CREATE THE UNIVERSE;**
& Spot the Alpha

JEWEL PROCEDURE—PART 4

[*Spot the "object-item" to get the reads. For each item-line: spot the proper number of objects, in the proper positions, with the proper motion taking place, in order to get the best "reads" until that action no longer registers on the Meter. A Seeker may wish to prepare simple diagrams of the shapes/objects on their worksheet, including arrows to indicate the motion (either coming towards or going away).*]

4.1.0 *Spot the Light; Spot the Alpha*

4.1.1 *Spot one transparent* **TRIANGLE** *going away from the front.*

4.1.2 *Spot two transparent* **TRIANGLES** *going away from the sides.*

4.1.3 *Spot three transparent* **TRIANGLES** *going away from the sides and the front.*

4.1.4 *Spot four transparent* **TRIANGLES** *going away from the front, back, and sides.*

4.2.1 *Spot one transparent* **TRIANGLE** *coming in from the front.*

4.2.2 *Spot two transparent* **TRIANGLES** *coming in from the sides.*

4.2.3 *Spot three transparent* **TRIANGLES** *coming in from the sides and the front.*

4.2.4 *Spot four transparent* **TRIANGLES** *coming in from the front, back, and sides.*

4.3.0 *Spot the Light; Spot the Alpha*

4.3.1 *Spot one transparent* CIRCLE
going away from the front.

4.3.2 *Spot two transparent* CIRCLES
going away from the sides.

4.3.3 *Spot three transparent* CIRCLES
*going away from the sides and
the front.*

4.3.4 *Spot four transparent* CIRCLES
*going away from the front, back,
and sides.*

4.4.1 *Spot one transparent* CIRCLE
coming in from the front.

4.4.2 *Spot two transparent* CIRCLES
coming in from the sides.

4.4.3 *Spot three transparent* CIRCLES
*coming in from the sides and
the front.*

4.4.4 *Spot four transparent* CIRCLES
*coming in from the front, back,
and sides.*

4.5.0 *Spot the Light; Spot the Alpha*

4.5.1 *Spot one transparent* SQUARE
going away from the front.

4.5.2 *Spot two transparent* SQUARES
going away from the sides.

4.5.3 *Spot three transparent* SQUARES
*going away from the sides and
the front.*

4.5.4 *Spot four transparent* SQUARES
*going away from the front, back,
and sides.*

4.6.1 *Spot one transparent* SQUARE
coming in from the front.

4.6.2 *Spot two transparent* SQUARES
coming in from the sides.

4.6.3 *Spot three transparent* SQUARES
*coming in from the sides and
the front.*

4.6.4 *Spot four transparent* SQUARES
*coming in from the front, back,
and sides.*

4.7.0 *Spot the Light; Spot the Alpha*

4.7.1 *Spot one transparent* OVAL *going
away from the front.*

4.7.2 *Spot two transparent* OVALS
going away from the sides.

4.7.3 *Spot three transparent* **OVALS** *going away from the sides and the front.*

4.7.4 *Spot four transparent* **OVALS** *going away from the front, back, and sides.*

4.8.1 *Spot one transparent* **OVAL** *coming in from the front.*

4.8.2 *Spot two transparent* **OVALS** *coming in from the sides.*

4.8.3 *Spot three transparent* **OVALS** *coming in from the sides and the front.*

4.8.4 *Spot four transparent* **OVALS** *coming in from the front, back, and sides.*

4.9.0 *Spot the Light; Spot the Alpha*

4.9.1 *Spot one transparent* **TETRAHEDRON** *going away from the front.*

4.9.2 *Spot two transparent* **TETRAHEDRONS** *going away from the sides.*

4.9.3 *Spot three transparent* **TETRAHEDRONS** *going away from the sides and the front.*

4.9.4 *Spot four transparent* **TETRAHEDRONS** *going away from the front, back, and sides.*

4.10.1 *Spot one transparent* **TETRAHEDRON** *coming in from the front.*

4.10.2 *Spot two transparent* **TETRAHEDRONS** *coming in from the sides.*

4.10.3 *Spot three transparent* **TETRAHEDRONS** *coming in from the sides and the front.*

4.10.4 *Spot four transparent* **TETRAHEDRONS** *coming in from the front, back, and sides.*

4.11.0 *Spot the Light; Spot the Alpha*

4.11.1 *Spot one transparent* **SPHERE** *going away from the front.*

4.11.2 *Spot two transparent* **SPHERES** *going away from the sides.*

4.11.3 *Spot three transparent* **SPHERES** *going away from the sides and the front.*

4.11.4 *Spot four transparent* **SPHERES** *going away from the front, back, and sides.*

4.12.1 *Spot one transparent* **SPHERE** *coming in from the front.*

4.12.2 *Spot two transparent* **SPHERES** *coming in from the sides.*

4.12.3 *Spot three transparent* **SPHERES** *coming in from the sides and the front.*

4.12.4 *Spot four transparent* **SPHERES** *coming in from the front, back, and sides.*

4.13.0 *Spot the Light; Spot the Alpha*

4.13.1 *Spot one transparent* **CUBE** *going away from the front.*

4.13.2 *Spot two transparent* **CUBES** *going away from the sides.*

4.13.3 *Spot three transparent* **CUBES** *going away from the sides and the front.*

4.13.4 *Spot four transparent* **CUBES** *going away from the front, back, and sides.*

4.14.1 *Spot one transparent* **CUBE** *coming in from the front.*

4.14.2 *Spot two transparent* **CUBES** *coming in from the sides.*

4.14.3 *Spot three transparent* **CUBES** *coming in from the sides and the front.*

4.14.4 *Spot four transparent* **CUBES** *coming in from the front, back, and sides.*

4.15.0 *Spot the Light; Spot the Alpha*

4.15.1 *Spot one transparent* **EGG** *going away from the front.*

4.15.2 *Spot two transparent* **EGGS** *going away from the sides.*

4.15.3 *Spot three transparent* **EGGS** *going away from the sides and the front.*

4.15.4 *Spot four transparent* **EGGS** *going away from the front, back, and sides.*

4.16.1 *Spot one transparent* **EGG** *coming in from the front.*

4.16.2 *Spot two transparent* **EGGS** *coming in from the sides.*

4.16.3 *Spot three transparent* **EGGS** *coming in from the sides and the front.*

4.16.4 *Spot four transparent* **EGGS** *coming in from the front, back, and sides.*

4.17.0 *Spot the Light; Spot the Alpha*

4.17.1 *Spot one transparent* **PRISM** *going away from the front.*

4.17.2 *Spot two transparent* **PRISMS** *going away from the sides.*

4.17.3 *Spot three transparent* **PRISMS** *going away from the sides and the front.*

4.17.4 *Spot four transparent* **PRISMS** *going away from the front, back, and sides.*

4.18.1 *Spot one transparent* **PRISM** *coming in from the front.*

4.18.2 *Spot two transparent* **PRISMS** *coming in from the sides.*

4.18.3 *Spot three transparent* **PRISMS** *coming in from the sides and the front.*

4.18.4 *Spot four transparent* **PRISMS** *coming in from the front, back, and sides.*

4.19.0 *Spot the Light; Spot the Alpha*

4.19.1 *Spot one transparent* **CYLINDER TUBE** *going away from the front.*

4.19.2 *Spot two transparent* **CYLINDER TUBES** *going away from the sides.*

4.19.3 *Spot three transparent* **CYLINDER TUBES** *going away from the sides and the front.*

4.19.4 *Spot four transparent* **CYLINDER TUBES** *going away from the front, back, and sides.*

4.20.1 *Spot one transparent* **CYLINDER TUBE** *coming in from the front.*

4.20.2 *Spot two transparent* **CYLINDER TUBES** *coming in from the sides.*

4.20.3 *Spot three transparent* **CYLINDER TUBES** *coming in from the sides and the front.*

4.20.4 *Spot four transparent* **CYLINDER TUBES** *coming in from the front, back, and sides.*

4.21.0 *Spot the Light; Spot the Alpha*

4.21.1 *Spot one transparent* **RECTANGULAR BOX** *going away from the front.*

4.21.2 *Spot two transparent* **RECTANGULAR BOXES** *going away from the sides.*

4.21.3 *Spot three transparent*
        RECTANGULAR BOXES *going*
        away from the sides and the front.

4.21.4 *Spot four transparent*
        RECTANGULAR BOXES *going*
        away from the front, back
        and sides.

4.22.1 *Spot one transparent*
        RECTANGULAR BOX *coming in*
        from the front.

4.22.2 *Spot two transparent*
        RECTANGULAR BOXES *coming*
        in from the sides.

4.22.3 *Spot three transparent*
        RECTANGULAR BOXES *coming*
        in from the sides and the front.

4.22.4 *Spot four transparent*
        RECTANGULAR BOXES *coming*
        in from the front, back, and sides.

4.23.0 *Spot the Light; Spot the Alpha*

4.23.1 *Spot one transparent* FLATTENED
        TUBE *going away from the front.*

4.23.2 *Spot two transparent* FLATTENED TUBES *going away from the sides.*

4.23.3 *Spot three transparent* FLATTENED TUBES *going away from the sides and the front.*

4.23.4 *Spot four transparent* FLATTENED TUBES *going away from the front, back, and sides.*

4.24.1 *Spot one transparent* FLATTENED TUBE *coming in from the front.*

4.24.2 *Spot two transparent* FLATTENED TUBES *coming in from the sides.*

4.24.3 *Spot three transparent* FLATTENED TUBES *coming in from the sides and the front.*

4.24.4 *Spot four transparent* FLATTENED TUBES *coming in from the front, back, and sides.*

4.25.0 *Spot the Light; Spot the Alpha*

4.25.1 *Spot one transparent* PYRAMID *going away from the front.*

4.25.2 *Spot two transparent* **PYRAMIDS**
going away from the sides.

4.25.3 *Spot three transparent* **PYRAMIDS**
going away from the sides and
the front.

4.25.4 *Spot four transparent* **PYRAMIDS**
going away from the front, back,
and sides.

4.26.1 *Spot one transparent* **PYRAMID**
coming in from the front.

4.26.2 *Spot two transparent* **PYRAMIDS**
coming in from the sides.

4.26.3 *Spot three transparent* **PYRAMIDS**
coming in from the sides and
the front.

4.26.4 *Spot four transparent* **PYRAMIDS**
coming in from the front, back,
and sides.

4.27.0 *Spot the Light; Spot the Alpha*

4.27.1 *Spot one transparent* **COIL** *going*
away from the front.

4.27.2 *Spot two transparent* **COILS** *going*
away from the sides.

4.27.3 *Spot three transparent* **COILS**
        going away from the sides and
        the front.

4.27.4 *Spot four transparent* **COILS**
        going away from the front, back,
        and sides.

4.28.1 *Spot one transparent* **COIL** *coming*
        in from the front.

4.28.2 *Spot two transparent* **COILS**
        coming in from the sides.

4.28.3 *Spot three transparent* **COILS**
        coming in from the sides and
        the front.

4.28.4 *Spot four transparent* **COILS**
        coming in from the front, back,
        and sides.

4.29.0 *Spot the Light; Spot the Alpha*

4.29.1 *Spot one transparent* **DIAMOND**
        BOX *going away from the front.*

4.29.2 *Spot two transparent* **DIAMOND**
        BOXES *going away from*
        the sides.

4.29.3 *Spot three transparent* **DIAMOND BOXES** *going away from the sides and the front.*

4.29.4 *Spot four transparent* **DIAMOND BOXES** *going away from the front, back, and sides.*

4.30.1 *Spot one transparent* **DIAMOND BOX** *coming in from the front.*

4.30.2 *Spot two transparent* **DIAMOND BOXES** *coming in from the sides.*

4.30.3 *Spot three transparent* **DIAMOND BOXES** *coming in from the sides and the front.*

4.30.4 *Spot four transparent* **DIAMOND BOXES** *coming in from the front, back, and sides.*

4.31.0 *Spot the Light; Spot the Alpha*

4.31.1 *Spot one transparent* **OVAL COIL TUBE** *going away from the front.*

4.31.2 *Spot two transparent* **OVAL COIL TUBES** *going away from the sides.*

4.31.3 *Spot three transparent* **OVAL COIL TUBES** *going away from the sides and the front.*

4.31.4 *Spot four transparent* **OVAL COIL TUBES** *going away from the front, back, and sides.*

4.32.1 *Spot one transparent* **OVAL COIL TUBE** *coming in from the front.*

4.32.2 *Spot two transparent* **OVAL COIL TUBES** *coming in from the sides.*

4.32.3 *Spot three transparent* **OVAL COIL TUBES** *coming in from the sides and the front.*

4.32.4 *Spot four transparent* **OVAL COIL TUBES** *coming in from the front, back, and sides.*

JEWEL PROCEDURE—PART 5

[*Spot the "object-item" to get the reads. For each item-line: spot the proper number of objects, in the proper positions, with the pro-*

*proper motion taking place, in order to get
the best "reads" until that action no longer
registers on the Meter. A Seeker may wish to
prepare simple diagrams of the shapes/objects
on their worksheet, including arrows to
indicate the motion (either coming towards or
going away). When you complete this, return
to Part-1 until you have completed a series of
ten full cycles.]*

5.1.0 *Spot the Light; Spot the Alpha*

5.1.1 *Spot one solid* **TRIANGLE** *going
away from the front.*

5.1.2 *Spot two solid* **TRIANGLES** *going
away from the sides.*

5.1.3 *Spot three solid* **TRIANGLES**
*going away from the sides and
the front.*

5.1.4 *Spot four solid* **TRIANGLES** *going
away from the front, back,
and sides.*

5.2.1 *Spot one solid* **TRIANGLE** *coming
in from the front.*

5.2.2 *Spot two solid* **TRIANGLES**
       coming in from the sides.

5.2.3 *Spot three solid* **TRIANGLES**
       coming in from the sides and
       the front.

5.2.4 *Spot four solid* **TRIANGLES**
       coming in from the front, back,
       and sides.

5.3.0 *Spot the Light; Spot the Alpha*

5.3.1 *Spot one solid* **CIRCLE** *going*
       away from the front.

5.3.2 *Spot two solid* **CIRCLES** *going*
       away from the sides.

5.3.3 *Spot three solid* **CIRCLES** *going*
       away from the sides and the front.

5.3.4 *Spot four solid* **CIRCLES** *going*
       away from the front, back,
       and sides.

5.4.1 *Spot one solid* **CIRCLE** *coming in*
       from the front.

5.4.2 *Spot two solid* **CIRCLES** *coming*
       in from the sides.

5.4.3 *Spot three solid* **CIRCLES** *coming in from the sides and the front.*

5.4.4 *Spot four solid* **CIRCLES** *coming in from the front, back, and sides.*

5.5.0 *Spot the Light; Spot the Alpha*

5.5.1 *Spot one solid* **SQUARE** *going away from the front.*

5.5.2 *Spot two solid* **SQUARES** *going away from the sides.*

5.5.3 *Spot three solid* **SQUARES** *going away from the sides and the front.*

5.5.4 *Spot four solid* **SQUARES** *going away from the front, back, and sides.*

5.6.1 *Spot one solid* **SQUARE** *coming in from the front.*

5.6.2 *Spot two solid* **SQUARES** *coming in from the sides.*

5.6.3 *Spot three solid* **SQUARES** *coming in from the sides and the front.*

5.6.4 *Spot four solid* **SQUARES** *coming in from the front, back, and sides.*

5.7.0   *Spot the Light; Spot the Alpha*

5.7.1   *Spot one solid* **OVAL** *going away from the front.*

5.7.2   *Spot two solid* **OVALS** *going away from the sides.*

5.7.3   *Spot three solid* **OVALS** *going away from the sides and the front.*

5.7.4   *Spot four solid* **OVALS** *going away from the front, back, and sides.*

5.8.1   *Spot one solid* **OVAL** *coming in from the front.*

5.8.2   *Spot two solid* **OVALS** *coming in from the sides.*

5.8.3   *Spot three solid* **OVALS** *coming in from the sides and the front.*

5.8.4   *Spot four solid* **OVALS** *coming in from the front, back, and sides.*

5.9.0   *Spot the Light; Spot the Alpha*

5.9.1   *Spot one solid* **TETRAHEDRON** *going away from the front.*

5.9.2   *Spot two solid* **TETRAHEDRONS** *going away from the sides.*

5.9.3 *Spot three solid* **TETRAHEDRONS** *going away from the sides and the front.*

5.9.4 *Spot four solid* **TETRAHEDRONS** *going away from the front, back, and sides.*

5.10.1 *Spot one solid* **TETRAHEDRON** *coming in from the front.*

5.10.2 *Spot two solid* **TETRAHEDRONS** *coming in from the sides.*

5.10.3 *Spot three solid* **TETRAHEDRONS** *coming in from the sides and the front.*

5.10.4 *Spot four solid* **TETRAHEDRONS** *coming in from the front, back, and sides.*

5.11.0 *Spot the Light; Spot the Alpha*

5.11.1 *Spot one solid* **SPHERE** *going away from the front.*

5.11.2 *Spot two solid* **SPHERES** *going away from the sides.*

5.11.3 *Spot three solid* **SPHERES** *going away from the sides and the front.*

5.11.4 *Spot four solid* **SPHERES** *going away from the front, back, and sides.*

5.12.1 *Spot one solid* **SPHERE** *coming in from the front.*

5.12.2 *Spot two solid* **SPHERES** *coming in from the sides.*

5.12.3 *Spot three solid* **SPHERES** *coming in from the sides and the front.*

5.12.4 *Spot four solid* **SPHERES** *coming in from the front, back, and sides.*

5.13.0 *Spot the Light; Spot the Alpha*

5.13.1 *Spot one solid* **CUBE** *going away from the front.*

5.13.2 *Spot two solid* **CUBES** *going away from the sides.*

5.13.3 *Spot three solid* **CUBES** *going away from the sides and the front.*

5.13.4 *Spot four solid* **CUBES** *going away from the front, back, and sides.*

5.14.1 *Spot one solid* **CUBE** *coming in from the front.*

5.14.2 *Spot two solid* **CUBES** *coming in from the sides.*

5.14.3 *Spot three solid* **CUBES** *coming in from the sides and the front.*

5.14.4 *Spot four solid* **CUBES** *coming in from the front, back, and sides.*

5.15.0 *Spot the Light; Spot the Alpha*

5.15.1 *Spot one solid* **EGG** *going away from the front.*

5.15.2 *Spot two solid* **EGGS** *going away from the sides.*

5.15.3 *Spot three solid* **EGGS** *going away from the sides and the front.*

5.15.4 *Spot four solid* **EGGS** *going away from the front, back, and sides.*

5.16.1 *Spot one solid* **EGG** *coming in from the front.*

5.16.2 *Spot two solid* **EGGS** *coming in from the sides.*

5.16.3 *Spot three solid* **EGGS** *coming in from the sides and the front.*

5.16.4 *Spot four solid* **EGGS** *coming in from the front, back, and sides.*

5.17.0 *Spot the Light; Spot the Alpha*

5.17.1 *Spot one solid* **PRISM** *going away from the front.*

5.17.2 *Spot two solid* **PRISMS** *going away from the sides.*

5.17.3 *Spot three solid* **PRISMS** *going away from the sides and the front.*

5.17.4 *Spot four solid* **PRISMS** *going away from the front, back, and sides.*

5.18.1 *Spot one solid* **PRISM** *coming in from the front.*

5.18.2 *Spot two solid* **PRISMS** *coming in from the sides.*

5.18.3 *Spot three solid* **PRISMS** *coming in from the sides and the front.*

5.18.4 *Spot four solid* **PRISMS** *coming in from the front, back, and sides.*

5.19.0 *Spot the Light; Spot the Alpha*

5.19.1 *Spot one solid* CYLINDER TUBE *going away from the front.*

5.19.2 *Spot two solid* CYLINDER TUBES *going away from the sides.*

5.19.3 *Spot three solid* CYLINDER TUBES *going away from the sides and the front.*

5.19.4 *Spot four solid* CYLINDER TUBES *going away from the front, back, and sides.*

5.20.1 *Spot one solid* CYLINDER TUBE *coming in from the front.*

5.20.2 *Spot two solid* CYLINDER TUBES *coming in from the sides.*

5.20.3 *Spot three solid* CYLINDER TUBES *coming in from the sides and the front.*

5.20.4 *Spot four solid* CYLINDER TUBES *coming in from the front, back, and sides.*

5.21.0 *Spot the Light; Spot the Alpha*

5.21.1 *Spot one solid* RECTANGULAR BOX *going away from the front.*

5.21.2   *Spot two solid* **RECTANGULAR BOXES** *going away from the sides.*

5.21.3   *Spot three solid* **RECTANGULAR BOXES** *going away from the sides and the front.*

5.21.4   *Spot four solid* **RECTANGULAR BOXES** *going away from the front, back, and sides.*

5.22.1   *Spot one solid* **RECTANGULAR BOX** *coming in from the front.*

5.22.2   *Spot two solid* **RECTANGULAR BOXES** *coming in from the sides.*

5.22.3   *Spot three solid* **RECTANGULAR BOXES** *coming in from the sides and the front.*

5.22.4   *Spot four solid* **RECTANGULAR BOXES** *coming in from the front, back, and sides.*

5.23.0   *Spot the Light; Spot the Alpha*

5.23.1   *Spot one solid* **FLATTENED TUBE** *going away from the front.*

5.23.2 *Spot two solid* **FLATTENED TUBES** *going away from the sides.*

5.23.3 *Spot three solid* **FLATTENED TUBES** *going away from the sides and the front.*

5.23.4 *Spot four solid* **FLATTENED TUBES** *going away from the front, back, and sides.*

5.24.1 *Spot one solid* **FLATTENED TUBE** *coming in from the front.*

5.24.2 *Spot two solid* **FLATTENED TUBES** *coming in from the sides.*

5.24.3 *Spot three solid* **FLATTENED TUBES** *coming in from the sides and the front.*

5.24.4 *Spot four solid* **FLATTENED TUBES** *coming in from the front, back, and sides.*

5.25.0 *Spot the Light; Spot the Alpha*

5.25.1 *Spot one solid* **PYRAMID** *going away from the front.*

5.25.2 *Spot two solid* **PYRAMIDS** *going away from the sides.*

5.25.3 *Spot three solid* **PYRAMIDS** *going away from the sides and the front.*

5.25.4 *Spot four solid* **PYRAMIDS** *going away from the front, back, and sides.*

5.26.1 *Spot one solid* **PYRAMID** *coming in from the front.*

5.26.2 *Spot two solid* **PYRAMIDS** *coming in from the sides.*

5.26.3 *Spot three solid* **PYRAMIDS** *coming in from the sides and the front.*

5.26.4 *Spot four solid* **PYRAMIDS** *coming in from the front, back, and sides.*

5.27.0 *Spot the Light; Spot the Alpha*

5.27.1 *Spot one solid* **COIL** *going away from the front.*

5.27.2 *Spot two solid* **COILS** *going away from the sides.*

5.27.3 *Spot three solid* **COILS** *going away from the sides and the front.*

5.27.4 *Spot four solid* **COILS** *going away from the front, back, and sides.*

5.28.1 *Spot one solid* **COIL** *coming in from the front.*

5.28.2 *Spot two solid* **COILS** *coming in from the sides.*

5.28.3 *Spot three solid* **COILS** *coming in from the sides and the front.*

5.28.4 *Spot four solid* **COILS** *coming in from the front, back, and sides.*

5.29.0 *Spot the Light; Spot the Alpha*

5.29.1 *Spot one solid* **DIAMOND BOX** *going away from the front.*

5.29.2 *Spot two solid* **DIAMOND BOXES** *going away from the sides.*

5.29.3 *Spot three solid* **DIAMOND BOXES** *going away from the sides and the front.*

5.29.4 *Spot four solid* **DIAMOND BOXES** *going away from the front, back, and sides.*

5.30.1 *Spot one solid* **DIAMOND BOX** *coming in from the front.*

5.30.2 *Spot two solid* **DIAMOND BOXES** *coming in from the sides.*

5.30.3 *Spot three solid* **DIAMOND BOXES** *coming in from the sides and the front.*

5.30.4 *Spot four solid* **DIAMOND BOXES** *coming in from the front, back, and sides.*

5.31.0 *Spot the Light; Spot the Alpha*

5.31.1 *Spot one solid* **OVAL COIL TUBE** *going away from the front.*

5.31.2 *Spot two solid* **OVAL COIL TUBES** *going away from the sides.*

5.31.3 *Spot three solid* **OVAL COIL TUBES** *going away from the sides and the front.*

5.31.4 *Spot four solid* **OVAL COIL TUBES** *going away from the front, back, and sides.*

5.32.1 *Spot one solid* **OVAL COIL TUBE** *coming in from the front.*

5.32.2 *Spot two solid* **OVAL COIL TUBES** *coming in from the sides.*

5.32.3 *Spot three solid* **OVAL COIL TUBES** *coming in from the sides and the front.*

5.32.4 *Spot four solid* **OVAL COIL TUBES** *coming in from the front, back, and sides.*

LEVEL-7 STABILIZATION POINT

Having completed *"The Jewel" Procedure*, a *Seeker* will likely have been *in-session* for several months, intensely handling a particular *Implanting-Incident* from a very long time ago. It is now time to "stabilize" these *gains* by bringing *Awareness* off of the *Backtrack (Spiritual Timeline)* and establishing *presence* in *present-time* again. To accomplish this, we will apply light *objective exercises*.

These *exercises* are all practiced outdoors, preferably during the day and in wide-open public places, such as a "park." Some do not require that environment and may be done "closer to home" or "alone" where appropriate. The purpose of this *Level-7 Stabilization Point* is to "extravert" a *Seeker's Awareness*, now that *"The Jewel" Procedure* is complete—rather than dwelling on the procedure or feeling introversion from months of *intensive processing.*

As a procedure or regimen, this series of exercises is similar to a "treasure hunt," except instead of collecting things, a *Seeker* goes out and walks around *spotting* and *noticing* various things. While these exercises may seem fairly casual, to remain systematic: a *Seeker* should distinguish a definitive "start-point" and "end-point" for each *processing exercise.*

Suitable *end-points* for an exercise include: feeling "brighter" or "better" (as a result of the exercise); having a "new realization" of any kind; gaining an increase in "spiritual perception"; assuming an "exterior viewpoint" (such as ZU-Vision); or if there have been no significant changes while processing for 15-20 minutes.

This first exercise is called "*New Discover-*

ies"—and unlike the others that follow, it is a PCL-series that is repeatedly *run* sequentially—1, 2, 3, 4, 5, 1, 2,...until a satisfactory *end-point*. [To be effective: it is important to actually *spot* and *identify* "some thing" and then *notice* "something about it"—rather than just darting around your attention and barely glancing at things.]

1. *"Spot some thing 'small'; notice something about it."*

2. *"Spot some thing 'big'; notice something about it."*

3. *"Spot some thing 'near'; notice something about it."*

4. *"Spot some thing 'far'; notice something about it."*

5. *"Spot some thing 'interesting'; notice something about it."*

Now that the *Seeker* has loosened up their *attention*: the following *objective exercises* may be combined or treated individually, depending on one's *session-time*, progress, and the availability of an appropriate (and safe) environment.

A. *"Look around; count all the 'bodies' that you see. Then walk around and count some more. Keep track of how many you counted."*

B. *"Look around; count all the 'female bodies' that you see. Notice something about each of them. Then walk around and count some more, noticing something about each of them."*

C. *"Look around; count all the 'male bodies' that you see. Notice something about each of them. Then walk around and count some more, noticing something about each of them."*

D. *"Locate a 'crowd' of human bodies. Spot the 'crowd' for its 'mass'; notice something about it. Spot the 'crowd' for the 'individuals'; notice something about it. Then alternate: Spotting the crowd as a mass; Spotting the crowd as individuals."*

E. *"Observe people and your surroundings. Alternate: Spot objects you are not; Spot people you are not. Spot objects you are separate from; Spot people you are separate from."*

F. *"Walk around and observe people and your surroundings. Alternate: Spot a person walking towards you; notice something about it. Spot a person walking away from you; notice something about it."*

G. *"Walk around and observe people. Spot 'bodies' for their 'mass'; notice how they are 'anchored' to the ground."*

H. *"Spot something (physical) about yourself that you don't like. Now observe other people and notice something about that part of them."*

I. *"Look around and spot a 'body'. Get the sense that an 'Alpha-Spirit' is operating it. Do this many times."*

IMPLANTS AFTER "THE JEWEL"

An *advanced Seeker* has come a long way on the *Pathway* by this level of work. Having completed *"The Jewel" Procedure* —and taken a few weeks to reorient themselves in present-time with the *objective exercises* in the previous section— they are then ready to continue.

There are many areas that a *Seeker* "could" now pursue—including other *"False Jewel" incidents*, such as discussed in *AT Manual #4, "Implanted Universes."* But, for present purposes, *Systemology Level-7* is primarily concerned with *Implants* that have most strongly *solidified* and *fragmented* the *reality-agreements* and *programming* inherent to being "imprisoned" or "entrapped" in *this Physical Universe*.

This part of our progress gets a little more complicated; because some of the "*charge*" on these other *Implant-Items* does not always belong to us directly—but is held by other "*entities*" and "*spiritual fragments.*"

Although such subjects ("*entities,*" &tc.) are not addressed fully until *Systemology Level-8*: an *advanced Seeker* that has effectively handled "*The Jewel*" and "*Heaven Incident*" is experienced and skilled enough to "*discharge*" other related *Implants.*

Because we are dealing with *Alpha-Defragmentation*—and a composite situation where we are often connected to other *entities* during shared *incidents*—the methods of previous *processing-levels* are not appropriate or effective for these *eighteen Implant-Platforms.*

These *entities* often remain in close "proximity" to us during our lives after receiving the same *Implanting* we did. Some of them actually believe they *are* "us." By handling these *Implants* now at this level, a *Seeker* will find *Systemology Level-8* to be much more understandable and effective.

Use only the techniques and instruction from *"The Jewel" Implant-Procedure*, and the other eighteen *Implant-Platforms* within this current manual. The same rules apply; except that a *Seeker* has gotten used to *"spotting the Light"* as the hypnotic-mechanism. Most of these additional *Implant-Platforms* employed some other similar event (as the *"Light"*) to confuse the *Alpha-Spirit* and/or reinforce the significance of its message. It could be *"explosions," "electrical shocks"* or even *"moving suns"* (to provide an illusion of time passing).

As with *"seeing the Light"* (as a *visualization*), it is *not* necessary to *"hear an explosion," "feel a shock,"* or *"see a moving sun"* in order to *"spot"* and *"contact"* it. Although that part is not verbalized out loud as part of the "command-item," a

Seeker might say/intend "*Spot the explosion*" (*&tc.*) silently to themselves. When you "*spot*" *where* and *what* should be there, you get a *Meter-read*. Then, you keep *spotting* the *implant-item* that way until the action no longer *registers* a *charge*.

There is actually so much *charge* on these *Platforms* that it is not expected to be totally handled with a single *series-run*. It has been a standard practice among *advanced Seekers* to apply the same *ten-fold-Cycle* method from "*The Jewel*" to these remaining *Implant-Platforms*.

As with the previous procedure: a *Seeker* also needs to *spot* the *Alpha-Spirit*, or *Self* — getting a sense (or an "impression") for how we were at the actual time of the *Implant/Incident*. Just as the PCL of "*Spot the Alpha*" was previously combined with "*Spot the Light*" (even when not written as such), for these *Platforms*: a *Seeker* may be required to simultaneously "*Spot the Exp-*

losion & Spot the Alpha" or *"Spot the Electric Shock & Spot the Alpha"* (depending on the *Platform* being *run*).

Because of the sheer amount of data found within these *Platforms*—and repetitive *patterns* that require a lot of unnecessary space and expense to fully print out in this manual—some of these *Platforms* will be presented as *formulas* or *patterns*, along with a list of *"keywords"* or *"buttons"* used to fill in the "blanks" of the *formula*—so that the basic *pattern* may be applied to a number of different *"items"* in turn.

This is *not* an assessment activity; each combination of *formula* and *keyword* requires being *run* item by item as if it were all written out in long-form. In addition to making a *worksheet* for marking *Meterreads*, a *Seeker* may need to use a *Platformformula* and list of *keywords* to write out their own long-form version of the complete *Implant* before *processing* it. Some

Seekers even make writing out the *Implant* a part of their *defragmentation* routine, as a means of seeing it *"external"* to *Self*—or *Self* being *"exterior"* to it. [This is highly recommended if a *Seeker* attempts these types of procedures without assistance of a *Biofeedback Device.*]

PLATFORM #1

[*This is a Platform long-form. It uses an "electric shock" as its implanting-gimmick. This may have reinforced a postulate that 'Alpha-Spirits are electrical-beings'. For this platform, the "command-item" (word) and the "electric shock" are connected; where there are two words, the "shock" occurs with the second word (in this case, the word "no"). Say the "command-item" a few times, spot the electric shock, spot the Alpha-Spirit; then say the "command-item" while spotting the Alpha-Spirit. Perform this whatever way produces the best "reads" until that action no longer registers a 'charge' on the GSR-Meter.*]

1.1.1 CREATE {*electric shock*};
      & Spot the Alpha

1.1.2 CREATE NO {*electric shock*};
      & Spot the Alpha

1.1.3 CREATE {*electric shock*},
      CREATE NO {*electric shock*};
      & Spot the Alpha

1.2.1 DESTROY {*electric shock*};
      & Spot the Alpha

1.2.2 DESTROY NO {*electric shock*};
      & Spot the Alpha

1.2.3 DESTROY {*electric shock*},
      DESTROY NO {*electric shock*};
      & Spot the Alpha

1.3.1 LOVE {*electric shock*};
      & Spot the Alpha

1.3.2 LOVE NO {*electric shock*};
      & Spot the Alpha

1.3.3 LOVE {*electric shock*},
      LOVE NO {*electric shock*};
      & Spot the Alpha

1.4.1 HATE {*electric shock*};
      & Spot the Alpha

1.4.2 HATE NO {*electric shock*};
      & Spot the Alpha

1.4.3 HATE {*electric shock*},
      HATE NO {*electric shock*};
      & Spot the Alpha

1.5.1 BE {*electric shock*};
      & Spot the Alpha

1.5.2 BE NO {*electric shock*};
      & Spot the Alpha

1.5.3 BE {*electric shock*},
      BE NO {*electric shock*};
      & Spot the Alpha

1.6.1 DISOWN {*electric shock*};
      & Spot the Alpha

1.6.2 DISOWN NO {*electric shock*};
      & Spot the Alpha

1.6.3 DISOWN {*electric shock*},
      DISOWN NO {*electric shock*};
      & Spot the Alpha

1.7.1 USE {*electric shock*};
      & Spot the Alpha

1.7.2 USE NO {*electric shock*};
      & Spot the Alpha

1.7.3 USE {*electric shock*},
USE NO {*electric shock*};
& Spot the Alpha

1.8.1 CONDEMN {*electric shock*};
& Spot the Alpha

1.8.2 CONDEMN NO {*electric shock*};
& Spot the Alpha

1.8.3 CONDEMN {*electric shock*},
CONDEMN NO {*electric
shock*}; *& Spot the Alpha*

1.9.1 SEIZE {*electric shock*};
& Spot the Alpha

1.9.2 SEIZE NO {*electric shock*};
& Spot the Alpha

1.9.3 SEIZE {*electric shock*},
SEIZE NO {*electric shock*};
& Spot the Alpha

1.10.1 ESCAPE {*electric shock*};
& Spot the Alpha

1.10.2 ESCAPE NO {*electric shock*};
& Spot the Alpha

1.10.3 ESCAPE {*electric shock*},
ESCAPE NO {*electric shock*};
& Spot the Alpha

PLATFORM #2

[*This is a Platform long-form. It uses a "sun swing" as its implanting-gimmick. The "sun-star" swings in an arc in front of you, from left to right. This may have given the illusion of time passing. The "command-item" (word) and the "sun swing" action are connected; where there are two words, it occurs with the second word. Say the "command-item" a few times, spot the sun swing, spot the Alpha-Spirit; then say the "command-item" while spotting the Alpha-Spirit. Perform this whatever way produces the best "reads" until that action no longer registers a 'charge' on the GSR-Meter.*]

2.1.1 **CREATE** {*sun swings*};
       & Spot the Alpha

2.1.2 **CREATE NO** {*sun swings*};
       & Spot the Alpha

2.1.3 **CREATE** {*sun swings*},
       CREATE NO {*sun swings*};
       & Spot the Alpha

2.2.1 ABIDE {*sun swings*};
& Spot the Alpha

2.2.2 ABIDE NO {*sun swings*};
& Spot the Alpha

2.2.3 ABIDE {*sun swings*}, ABIDE NO
{*sun swings*}; *& Spot the Alpha*

2.3.1 ENJOY {*sun swings*};
& Spot the Alpha

2.3.2 ENJOY NO {*sun swings*};
& Spot the Alpha

2.3.3 ENJOY {*sun swings*},
ENJOY NO {*sun swings*};
& Spot the Alpha

2.4.1 WELCOME {*sun swings*};
& Spot the Alpha

2.4.2 WELCOME NO {*sun swings*};
& Spot the Alpha

2.4.3 WELCOME {*sun swings*},
WELCOME NO {*sun swings*};
& Spot the Alpha

2.5.1 SHARE {*sun swings*};
& Spot the Alpha

2.5.2 SHARE NO {*sun swings*};
& Spot the Alpha

2.5.3 SHARE {*sun swings*},
SHARE NO {*sun swings*};
& Spot the Alpha

2.6.1 KEEP {*sun swings*};
& Spot the Alpha

2.6.2 KEEP NO {*sun swings*};
& Spot the Alpha

2.6.3 KEEP {*sun swings*}, KEEP NO
{*sun swings*}; *& Spot the Alpha*

2.7.1 HOLD {*sun swings*};
& Spot the Alpha

2.7.2 HOLD NO {*sun swings*};
& Spot the Alpha

2.7.3 HOLD {*sun swings*}, HOLD NO
{*sun swings*}; *& Spot the Alpha*

2.8.1 EXPLOIT {*sun swings*};
& Spot the Alpha

2.8.2 EXPLOIT NO {*sun swings*};
& Spot the Alpha

2.8.3 EXPLOIT {*sun swings*},
EXPLOIT NO {*sun swings*};
& Spot the Alpha

2.9.1 CONDEMN {*sun swings*};
& Spot the Alpha

2.9.2 CONDEMN NO {*sun swings*};
& Spot the Alpha

2.9.3 CONDEMN {*sun swings*},
CONDEMN NO {*sun swings*};
& Spot the Alpha

2.10.1 SKIP {*sun swings*};
& Spot the Alpha

2.10.2 SKIP NO {*sun swings*};
& Spot the Alpha

2.10.3 SKIP {*sun swings*}, SKIP NO
{*sun swings*}; *& Spot the Alpha*

2.11.1 CONTINUE {*sun swings*};
& Spot the Alpha

2.11.2 CONTINUE NO {*sun swings*};
& Spot the Alpha

2.11.3 CONTINUE {*sun swings*},
CONTINUE NO {*sun swings*};
& Spot the Alpha

2.12.1 FORGET {*sun swings*};
& Spot the Alpha

2.12.2 FORGET NO {*sun swings*};
& Spot the Alpha

2.12.3 FORGET {*sun swings*}, FORGET NO {*sun swings*}; *& Spot the Alpha*

This next set of command-items were communicated during the Implant. They may "read" individually, or when combined, or both. Defragment whatever is there.

2.13.1 "THAT'S WHAT YOU GET FOR CREATING THIS UNIVERSE"; *& Spot the Alpha*

2.13.2 "GET OUT!"; *& Spot the Alpha*

2.13.3 "THAT'S WHAT YOU GET FOR CREATING THIS UNIVERSE", "GET OUT!"; *& Spot the Alpha*

PLATFORM #3

[*This is a Platform long-form. It uses an "explosion" as its implanting-gimmick. The "explosion" occurs at the start and end of the Implant. There is also the "appearance of a gigantic being in the sky." This "gigantic being" is presumably issuing the "command-items" or at the very least is representing them. Say the "command-item" a few times, and spot the Alpha-Spirit; then say the "command-item" while spotting the Alpha-Spirit. Perform this whatever way produces the best "reads" until that action no longer registers a 'charge' on the GSR-Meter.*]

3.0.1 *{spot an explosion};*
       & Spot the Alpha

3.0.2 *{spot the appearance of gigantic being in the sky};*
       & Spot the Alpha

3.1.1 YOU MUST SURVIVE;
       & Spot the Alpha

3.1.2 YOU MUSTN'T SURVIVE;
       & Spot the Alpha

3.1.3 YOU MUST SURVIVE, YOU MUSTN'T SURVIVE;
       & Spot the Alpha

3.2.1 YOU SHOULD SURVIVE;
       & Spot the Alpha

3.2.2 YOU SHOULDN'T SURVIVE;
       & Spot the Alpha

3.2.3 **YOU SHOULD SURVIVE,**
      YOU SHOULDN'T SURVIVE;
      & Spot the Alpha

3.3.1 **YOU CAN SURVIVE;**
      & Spot the Alpha

3.3.2 **YOU CAN'T SURVIVE;**
      & Spot the Alpha

3.3.3 **YOU CAN SURVIVE,**
      YOU CAN'T SURVIVE;
      & Spot the Alpha

For the next three sets: defragment both the "he" and "she" as separate command-items. Only one or the other has to give a "read" for an item-line, but both should be checked and discharged fully.

3.4.1 **S/HE MUST SURVIVE;**
      & Spot the Alpha

3.4.2 **S/HE MUSTN'T SURVIVE;**
      & Spot the Alpha

3.4.3 **S/HE MUST SURVIVE,**
      S/HE MUSTN'T SURVIVE;
      & Spot the Alpha

3.5.1 **S/HE SHOULD SURVIVE;**
& Spot the Alpha

3.5.2 **S/HE SHOULDN'T SURVIVE;**
& Spot the Alpha

3.5.3 **S/HE SHOULD SURVIVE,
S/HE SHOULDN'T SURVIVE;**
& Spot the Alpha

3.6.1 **S/HE CAN SURVIVE;**
& Spot the Alpha

3.6.2 **S/HE CAN'T SURVIVE;**
& Spot the Alpha

3.6.3 **S/HE CAN SURVIVE,
S/HE CAN'T SURVIVE;**
& Spot the Alpha

3.7.1 **THEY MUST SURVIVE;**
& Spot the Alpha

3.7.2 **THEY MUSTN'T SURVIVE;**
& Spot the Alpha

3.7.3 **THEY MUST SURVIVE,
THEY MUSTN'T SURVIVE;**
& Spot the Alpha

3.8.1 **THEY SHOULD SURVIVE;**
& Spot the Alpha

3.8.2 THEY SHOULDN'T SURVIVE;
& Spot the Alpha

3.8.3 THEY SHOULD SURVIVE,
THEY SHOULDN'T SURVIVE;
& Spot the Alpha

3.9.1 THEY CAN SURVIVE;
& Spot the Alpha

3.9.2 THEY CAN'T SURVIVE;
& Spot the Alpha

3.9.3 THEY CAN SURVIVE,
THEY CAN'T SURVIVE;
& Spot the Alpha

3.10.1 WE MUST SURVIVE;
& Spot the Alpha

3.10.2 WE MUSTN'T SURVIVE;
& Spot the Alpha

3.10.3 WE MUST SURVIVE,
WE MUSTN'T SURVIVE;
& Spot the Alpha

3.11.1 WE SHOULD SURVIVE;
& Spot the Alpha

3.11.2 WE SHOULDN'T SURVIVE;
& Spot the Alpha

3.11.3 WE SHOULD SURVIVE,
WE SHOULDN'T SURVIVE;
& Spot the Alpha

3.12.1 WE CAN SURVIVE;
& Spot the Alpha

3.12.2 WE CAN'T SURVIVE;
& Spot the Alpha

3.12.3 WE CAN SURVIVE,
WE CAN'T SURVIVE;
& Spot the Alpha

3.13.1 ALL MUST SURVIVE;
& Spot the Alpha

3.13.2 ALL MUSTN'T SURVIVE;
& Spot the Alpha

3.13.3 ALL MUST SURVIVE,
ALL MUSTN'T SURVIVE;
& Spot the Alpha

3.14.1 ALL SHOULD SURVIVE;
& Spot the Alpha

3.14.2 ALL SHOULDN'T SURVIVE;
& Spot the Alpha

3.14.3 ALL SHOULD SURVIVE,
ALL SHOULDN'T SURVIVE;
& Spot the Alpha

3.15.1 **ALL CAN SURVIVE;**
     & Spot the Alpha

3.15.2 **ALL CAN'T SURVIVE;**
     & Spot the Alpha

3.15.3 **ALL CAN SURVIVE,**
     ALL CAN'T SURVIVE;
     & Spot the Alpha

3.16.0 *{spot an explosion}*;
     & Spot the Alpha

PLATFORM #4

[*This is a Platform formula. It uses an "interior room" (such as of a house) as its implant-setting. There is a pattern of ten "command-items" for each of five "keywords." This means there are 50 total command-items. The last word of each item-line is blank. Words for items 1 through 8 of this Platform are: 1) CREATE, 2) VIEW, 3) EXIST, 4) KNOW, and 5) REMEMBER. For items 9 and 10, use: 1) CREATIONS, 2) VIEWS, 3) EXISTENCES, 4) KNOWNS and 5) MEMORIES.*

Run each item-line (1 through 10) until three no-reads with "Create" (or "Creations") and then start from the top using "View"/ "Views" and so on. A Seeker should make five separate worksheets.]

4.1.X I SHOULD ___; *& Spot the Alpha*

4.2.X I SHOULDN'T ___;
& Spot the Alpha

4.3.X I MUST ___; *& Spot the Alpha*

4.4.X I MUSTN'T ___;
& Spot the Alpha

4.5.X I DO ___; *& Spot the Alpha*

4.6.X I DON'T ___; *& Spot the Alpha*

4.7.X I CAN ___; *& Spot the Alpha*

4.8.X I CAN'T ___; *& Spot the Alpha*

4.9.X THERE ARE ___;
& Spot the Alpha

4.10.X THERE AREN'T ___;
& Spot the Alpha

PLATFORM #5

[*This is a Platform long-form. It uses a "fierce heavy explosion" as its implanting-gimmick. The "explosion" is accompanied by sensations of "burning pain" at the start of the Implant. This is followed by a lightning storm. The Implant is meant to induce indecision and insanity. There is no requirement for the "heavy explosion with burning pain" or the "storm" to give a Meter-read. Spot them at the beginning anyway; and if there is a "charge" registering, then take it to three "no-reads" as standard practice. Say the "command-item" out loud, and spot the Alpha-Spirit; then say the "command-item" while spotting the Alpha-Spirit. Perform this whatever way produces the best "reads" until that action no longer registers.*]

5.0.1 {*spot a fierce heavy explosion*};
     & Spot the Alpha

5.0.2 {*spot a lightning storm*};
     & Spot the Alpha

5.1.1 **TO DIE IS TO LIVE;**
& Spot the Alpha

5.1.2 **TO LIVE IS TO DIE;**
& Spot the Alpha

5.1.3 **TO DIE IS TO LIVE, TO LIVE IS TO DIE;** *& Spot the Alpha*

5.2.1 **TO SURRENDER IS TO VICTIMIZE;** *& Spot the Alpha*

5.2.2 **TO VICTIMIZE IS TO SURRENDER;** *& Spot the Alpha*

5.2.3 **TO SURRENDER IS TO VICTIMIZE, TO VICTIMIZE IS TO SURRENDER;**
& Spot the Alpha

5.3.1 **TO LOSE IS TO WIN;**
& Spot the Alpha

5.3.2 **TO WIN IS TO LOSE;**
& Spot the Alpha

5.3.3 **TO LOSE IS TO WIN, TO WIN IS TO LOSE;** *& Spot the Alpha*

5.4.1 **TO DESPAIR IS TO HOPE;**
& Spot the Alpha

5.4.2 **TO HOPE IS TO DESPAIR;**
& Spot the Alpha

5.4.3 TO DESPAIR IS TO HOPE,
TO HOPE IS TO DESPAIR;
& Spot the Alpha

5.5.1 TO BE IGNORANT IS TO
KNOW; *& Spot the Alpha*

5.5.2 TO KNOW IS TO BE
IGNORANT; *& Spot the Alpha*

5.5.3 TO BE IGNORANT IS TO
KNOW, TO KNOW IS TO BE
IGNORANT; *& Spot the Alpha*

5.6.1 TO BE STUPID IS TO BE
SMART; *& Spot the Alpha*

5.6.2 TO BE SMART IS TO BE
STUPID; *& Spot the Alpha*

5.6.3 TO BE STUPID IS TO BE
SMART, TO BE SMART IS TO
BE STUPID; *& Spot the Alpha*

5.7.1 TO DISAGREE IS TO AGREE;
& Spot the Alpha

5.7.2 TO AGREE IS TO DISAGREE;
& Spot the Alpha

5.7.3 TO DISAGREE IS TO AGREE,
TO AGREE IS TO DISAGREE;
& Spot the Alpha

5.8.1 TO DETEST IS TO GET;
& Spot the Alpha

5.8.2 TO GET IS TO DETEST;
& Spot the Alpha

5.8.3 TO DETEST IS TO GET,
TO GET IS TO DETEST;
& Spot the Alpha

5.9.1 TO HURT IS TO ENJOY;
& Spot the Alpha

5.9.2 TO ENJOY IS TO HURT;
& Spot the Alpha

5.9.3 TO HURT IS TO ENJOY,
TO ENJOY IS TO HURT;
& Spot the Alpha

5.10.1 TO DISLIKE IS TO LIKE;
& Spot the Alpha

5.10.2 TO LIKE IS TO DISLIKE;
& Spot the Alpha

5.10.3 TO DISLIKE IS TO LIKE,
TO LIKE IS TO DISLIKE;
& Spot the Alpha

5.11.1 TO HATE IS TO LOVE;
& Spot the Alpha

5.11.2 **TO LOVE IS TO HATE;**
& Spot the Alpha

5.11.3 **TO HATE IS TO LOVE,**
TO LOVE IS TO HATE;
& Spot the Alpha

5.12.1 **TO HINDER IS TO HELP;**
& Spot the Alpha

5.12.2 **TO HELP IS TO HINDER;**
& Spot the Alpha

5.12.3 **TO HINDER IS TO HELP,**
TO HELP IS TO HINDER;
& Spot the Alpha

5.13.1 **TO DISBELIEVE IS TO**
BELIEVE; *& Spot the Alpha*

5.13.2 **TO BELIEVE IS TO**
DISBELIEVE; *& Spot the Alpha*

5.13.3 **TO DISBELIEVE IS TO**
BELIEVE, TO BELIEVE IS TO
DISBELIEVE; *& Spot the Alpha*

5.14.1 **TO BE BAD IS TO BE GOOD;**
& Spot the Alpha

5.14.2 **TO BE GOOD IS TO BE BAD;**
& Spot the Alpha

5.14.3 TO BE BAD IS TO BE GOOD,
TO BE GOOD IS TO BE BAD;
& Spot the Alpha

5.15.1 TO BETRAY IS TO BE
FAITHFUL; *& Spot the Alpha*

5.15.2 TO BE FAITHFUL IS TO
BETRAY; *& Spot the Alpha*

5.15.3 TO BETRAY IS TO BE
FAITHFUL, TO BE FAITHFUL
IS TO BETRAY;
& Spot the Alpha

5.16.1 TO BE CRAZY IS TO BE
SANE; *& Spot the Alpha*

5.16.2 TO BE SANE IS TO BE
CRAZY; *& Spot the Alpha*

5.16.3 TO BE CRAZY IS TO BE
SANE, TO BE SANE IS TO BE
CRAZY; *& Spot the Alpha*

5.17.1 TO ABANDON IS TO
COLLECT; *& Spot the Alpha*

5.17.2 TO COLLECT IS TO
ABANDON; *& Spot the Alpha*

5.17.3 **TO ABANDON IS TO COLLECT, TO COLLECT IS TO ABANDON;** *& Spot the Alpha*

5.18.1 **TO STOP IS TO START;** *& Spot the Alpha*

5.18.2 **TO START IS TO STOP;** *& Spot the Alpha*

5.18.3 **TO STOP IS TO START, TO START IS TO STOP;** *& Spot the Alpha*

PLATFORM #6

[This is a Platform long-form. This incident starts with an "explosion" that knocks one unconscious prior to the Implant. This Implant artificially installs a foundation for false justifications (particularly for committing future harmful-acts). Although it is a long-form, it is actually used twice. The first time: run it as having put it over onto someone else. The second time: run it as though having received it from someone else. It begins and ends with the sense of being lost

in a whirlwind of electricity (which does not have to read when spotted, but if it registers, then it must be run to three "no-reads"). Say the "command-item" out loud, and spot the Alpha-Spirit; then say the "command-item" while spotting the Alpha-Spirit. Perform this whatever way produces the best "reads" until that action no longer registers.]

6.0.X *{spot a fierce electrical tornado};* & *Spot the Alpha*

6.1.X TO EXPERIENCE IS TO CREATE; & *Spot the Alpha*

6.2.X TO LOOK IS TO RE-ENVISION; & *Spot the Alpha*

6.3.X TO THINK IS TO RECALL; & *Spot the Alpha*

6.4.X TO CONCEIVE IS TO REMEMBER; & *Spot the Alpha*

6.5.X TO SEE IS TO FORGET; & *Spot the Alpha*

6.6.X *{spot a fierce electrical whirlwind};* & *Spot the Alpha*

PLATFORM #7

[*This is a Platform long-form. The incident is possible due to Platform #6; it provides a false illusion that you are Implanting someone else; then someone else is Implanting you. In actuality, you are sitting across from a "dummy-doll" and not another Alpha-Spirit. Additionally, you are sitting in front of a reflective screen. The implanting device is on your left. It directs an implanting-beam behind you onto the screen, which reflects onto the "dummy-doll" but giving you the impression that you did it.*

Although it is a long-form, it is actually used twice. The first time: run it as having a sense of doing it to someone else. The second time: run it as though having received it from someone else.

Say the "command-item" out loud, and spot the Alpha-Spirit; then say the "command-item" while spotting the Alpha-Spirit. Perform this whatever way produces the best "reads" until that action no longer registers.

For the italic environmental conditions; spot the occurrence or change and spot the Alpha until three consecutive no-reads.]

7.1.X {*a light appears to your left, the implanting device*};
& *Spot the Alpha*

7.2.X {*a light appears in front, the dummy-doll*}; & *Spot the Alpha*

7.3.X "NOW SLEEP—GO TO SLEEP"; & *Spot the Alpha*

7.4.X "YOU ARE UNCONSCIOUS";
& *Spot the Alpha*

7.5.X "YOU KNOW NOTHING";
& *Spot the Alpha*

7.6.X {*a gas pours into the area*};
& *Spot the Alpha*

7.7.X {*there is an impression of who implanted whom*};
& *Spot the Alpha*

PLATFORM #8

[This is a Platform long-form. The incident is possible due to Platform #7; it is a formal reprimand (or scolding) for having Implanted "our fellow Alpha-Spirit" (even though it was actually a dummy-doll and we really didn't do anything) and a warning about doing it again. The Implant installs the concept of "karma"—which is a reality-agreement (which did not exist in Home Universe). The entire contents are telepathically "spoken" to us. Each of the phrase-lines listed below will read as an item. Say each line out loud as a "command item" while spotting the Alpha (to three "no-reads") and then scan over the entire message (without spotting the Alpha) just to understand its general content.]

8.1 **"HERE IS A LESSON"**;
    & Spot the Alpha

8.2 **"IT IS"**; *& Spot the Alpha*

8.3 **"IF YOU DO SOMETHING TO ANOTHER"**; *& Spot the Alpha*

8.4 "THAT IS HARMFUL";
& Spot the Alpha

8.5 "OR DAMAGES HIM OR HER";
& Spot the Alpha

8.6 "IN ANY WAY"; *& Spot the Alpha*

8.7 "YOU GET IT BACK 100-FOLD";
& Spot the Alpha

8.8 "WITHOUT FAIL.";
& Spot the Alpha

8.9 "THIS IS YOUR ACTION TO ANOTHER"; *& Spot the Alpha*

8.10 "YOU ARE DOING THIS";
& Spot the Alpha

8.11 "TO A HELPLESS SPIRIT";
& Spot the Alpha

8.12 "WHO WAS GOOD AND KIND";
& Spot the Alpha

8.13 "IN ORDER TO RUIN THEM FOREVER"; *& Spot the Alpha*

8.14 "AND DEGRADE YOURSELF.";
& Spot the Alpha

8.15 "NOW WATCH THIS";
     & Spot the Alpha

8.16 "AND SEE WHAT YOU ARE
     DOING"; *& Spot the Alpha*

8.17 "TO HIM OR HER.";
     & Spot the Alpha

PLATFORM #9

[This is a Platform long-form. The incident is possible due to Platform #8; and like Platform #7, you are sitting across from a "dummy-doll" and not another Alpha-Spirit. Additionally, you are sitting in front of a reflective screen. The implanting device is on your left. It directs an implanting-beam behind you onto the screen, which reflects onto the "dummy-doll" but giving you the impression that you did it. Spot those environmental facets (the screen, device, beam, &tc.) throughout. Say the "command-item" out loud, and spot the Alpha-Spirit; then say the "command-item" while spotting the Alpha-Spirit. Perform this whatever way produces the best

"reads" until that action no longer registers (three consecutive times).]

9.0.1 {*spot an electrical explosion*}; *& Spot the Alpha*

9.1.1 TO PREDICT, NEVER TO KNOW; *& Spot the Alpha*

9.1.2 TO KNOW, NEVER TO PREDICT; *& Spot the Alpha*

9.2.1 TO FRIGHTEN, NEVER TO FEAR; *& Spot the Alpha*

9.2.2 TO FEAR, NEVER TO FRIGHTEN; *& Spot the Alpha*

9.3.1 TO CATCH, NEVER TO BE CAUGHT; *& Spot the Alpha*

9.3.2 TO BE CAUGHT, NEVER TO CATCH; *& Spot the Alpha*

9.4.1 TO IMPRISON, NEVER TO BE IMPRISONED; *& Spot the Alpha*

9.4.2 TO BE IMPRISONED, NEVER TO IMPRISON; *& Spot the Alpha*

9.5.1 TO BE OUT OF JAIL, NEVER TO BE IN JAIL; *& Spot the Alpha*

9.5.2 TO BE IN JAIL, NEVER TO BE OUT OF JAIL; *& Spot the Alpha*

9.6.1 **TO BE OUTSIDE, NEVER TO BE INSIDE;** *& Spot the Alpha*

9.6.2 **TO BE INSIDE, NEVER TO BE OUTSIDE;** *& Spot the Alpha*

9.7.1 **TO REMEMBER, NEVER TO FORGET;** *& Spot the Alpha*

9.7.2 **TO FORGET, NEVER TO REMEMBER;** *& Spot the Alpha*

9.8.1 **TO GO, NEVER TO COME;** *& Spot the Alpha*

9.8.2 **TO COME, NEVER TO GO;** *& Spot the Alpha*

9.9.1 **{*explosion*}**; *& Spot the Alpha*

PLATFORM #10

[*This is a Platform long-form. The incident is possible due to Platform #9; it is a formal reprimand (or scolding) for having Implanted "our fellow Alpha-Spirit" (even though it was actually a dummy-doll and we really didn't do anything). It is intended to reinforce mechanisms for retribution (motivations for harmful-acts). Its entire contents are tele-*

pathically "spoken" to us. Each of the phrase-lines listed below will read as an item. Say each line out loud as a "command item" while spotting the Alpha (to three "no-reads") and then scan over the entire content of the message (without spotting the Alpha).

You are still are opposite a dummy-doll; but now the reflective screen is behind them, projecting the implanting-beam toward you from their direction. Spot this environmental change before continuing. ("Spot the Alpha" will now be abbreviated as "&A.")]

10.1 "THE CONSEQUENCES"; *&A*

10.2 "OF YOUR HAVING DONE THAT"; *&A*

10.3 "ARE TERRIBLE,"; *&A*

10.4 "BECAUSE YOU DID THAT."; *& A*

10.5 "IT IS NOW TWO AND A HALF YEARS LATER."; *&A*

10.6 "THESE ARE THE CONSEQUENCES."; *&A*

10.7 "THIS IS THE CONSEQUENCE."; *&A*

10.8 "WATCH THIS"; *&A*

10.9 "AND SEE WHAT HAPPENS"; *&A*

10.10 "TO YOU"; *&A*

10.11 "BECAUSE OF WHAT YOU DID"; *&A*

10.12 "TO THE POOR SPIRIT."; *&A*

10.13 "THEY ARE NOW GIVING IT BACK."; *&A*

10.14 "WATCH OUT!"; *&A*

PLATFORM #11

[*This Platform is identical in content to Platform #9; except that it is run as being directed to us from someone else (the dummy-doll). A Seeker will have to make their own worksheet for its content, copying the data from Platform #9. It cannot be run in a series (or from a worksheet) as Platform #9, even though the content is the same. This is Platform #11.*

You are still are opposite a dummy-doll; the reflective screen is behind them, projecting the implanting-beam toward you from their direction. Say the "command-item" out loud, and spot the Alpha-Spirit; then say the "command-item" while spotting the Alpha-Spirit. Perform this whatever way produces the best "reads" until that action no longer registers (three consecutive times).]

PLATFORM #12

[This is a Platform long-form. The incident is possible due to Platform #10; it is a formal reminder of the retribution we have received from "our fellow Alpha-Spirit" (the dummy-doll, although it really came from an implanting device) as a result of implanting them first (although we actually didn't do anything). Each of the phrase-lines listed below will read as an item. Say each line out loud as a "command item" while spotting the Alpha (to three "no-reads") and then scan over the entire content of the message (without spot-

ting the Alpha). ("Spot the Alpha" will now be abbreviated as "&A.")]

12.1 "YOU SEE WHAT HAPPENS"; *&A*

12.2 "BECAUSE OF WHAT YOU DO."; *&A*

12.3 "WHEN YOU DO SOMETHING BAD"; *&A*

12.4 "TO ANOTHER"; *&A*

12.5 "YOU GET IT BACK LATER."; *&A*

12.6 "YOU ARE THE CAUSE"; *&A*

12.7 "OF ALL YOUR SUFFERING."; *&A*

12.8 "HARMFUL ACTIONS"; *&A*

12.9 "DO NOT PAY."; *&A*

12.10 "WAKE UP DEAD, FOREVER."; *&A*

PLATFORM #13

[*This is a Platform short-form formula. It contains a series of 26 "command-item" lines. This series (lines 1 through 26) is run completely for each of 26 different "keywords." Each word is used twice on each line. A Seeker should prepare 26 different worksheets from this formula, inserting only one keyword (of the 26) for each worksheet. This generates 676 different command-items. A Seeker must get three consecutive "no-reads" on a "keyword" by itself before running through the worksheet that uses it.*

To fully process-out this incident: once you have completed working through all 26 keywords/worksheets (676 items), the entire implant is run again in reverse, working backwards from its ending, line by line. Note that: here you work the lines in reverse order back up the worksheet pages (marking new "reads" in a different color), but you don't literally read a sentence backwards. Also note: some lines may not read. Whatever does, defragment it to three no-reads. Only backtrack if several lines in a row do not register a charge. Most of this implant is non-

sensical; don't analyze it, just defragment it. There is an "explosion" that occurs for each "command-item" that corresponds with "Spot the Alpha" because the "explosion" is actually taking place (or sensed) in the "head."]

KEYWORDS: 1) SELF; 2) MIND; 3) BODY; 4) SPIRIT; 5) HEAD; 6) MEMORY; 7) MASS; 8) THOUGHT; 9) UNIVERSE; 10) BELIEF; 11) PEOPLE; 12) INTENTION; 13) SOCIETY; 14) CUSTOM; 15) GOVERNMENT; 16) CONCEPT; 17) RELIGION; 18) COMPUTATION; 19) SYSTEM; 20) REASON; 21) HEALTH; 22) LOGIC; 23) POISON; 24) SECRET; 25) INTERIOR; 26) AMNESIA.

13.1.x STOP A BEGINNING ___ TO INVENT AN ENDED ___;
{explosion} & Spot the Alpha

13.2.x INVENT A NEAR ___ TO STOP A FAR ___; *{explosion} & Spot the Alpha*

13.3.x STOP AN OPEN ___ TO INVENT A CLOSED ___;
{explosion} & Spot the Alpha

13.4.x INVENT A KEPT ___ TO
STOP AN EXPENDED ___;
{explosion} & Spot the Alpha

13.5.x STOP A FILLED ___ TO
INVENT AN EXHAUSTED
___; *{explosion} &A*

13.6.x INVENT A BRIGHT ___ TO
STOP A DIM ___; *{explosion}
& Spot the Alpha*

13.7.x STOP AN INFORMED ___ TO
INVENT A DENIED ___;
{explosion} & Spot the Alpha

13.8.x INVENT A RECEIVING ___
TO STOP A REJECTED ___;
{explosion} & Spot the Alpha

13.9.x STOP A LOVING ___ TO
INVENT A HATED ___;
{explosion} & Spot the Alpha

13.10.x INVENT A PERCEIVING ___
TO STOP A BLINDED ___;
{explosion} & Spot the Alpha

13.11.x STOP A FAIR ___ TO INVENT
A PREJUDICED ___;
{explosion} & Spot the Alpha

13.12.x INVENT A CLEAN ___ TO
STOP A DIRTY ___;
{explosion} & Spot the Alpha

13.13.x STOP AN ARRIVING ___ TO
INVENT A DEPARTED ___;
{explosion} & Spot the Alpha

13.14.x INVENT AN ARRIVING ___
TO STOP A DEPARTED ___;
{explosion} & Spot the Alpha

13.15.x STOP A CLEAN ___ TO
INVENT A DIRTY ___;
{explosion} & Spot the Alpha

13.16.x INVENT A FAIR ___ TO STOP
A PREJUDICED ___;
{explosion} & Spot the Alpha

13.17.x STOP A PERCEIVING ___ TO
INVENT A BLINDED ___;
{explosion} & Spot the Alpha

13.18.x INVENT A LOVING ___ TO
STOP A HATED ___;
{explosion} & Spot the Alpha

13.19.x STOP A RECEIVING ___ TO
INVENT A REJECTED ___;
{explosion} & Spot the Alpha

13.20.X INVENT AN INFORMED ___
TO STOP A DENIED ___;
{explosion} & Spot the Alpha

13.21.X STOP A BRIGHT ___ TO
INVENT A DIM ___; *{explosion}*
& Spot the Alpha

13.22.X INVENT A FILLED ___ TO
STOP AN EXHAUSTED ___;
{explosion} & Spot the Alpha

13.23.X STOP A KEPT ___ TO
INVENT AN EXPENDED ___;
{explosion} & Spot the Alpha

13.24.X INVENT AN OPEN ___ TO
STOP A CLOSED ___;
{explosion} & Spot the Alpha

13.25.X STOP A NEAR ___ TO
INVENT A FAR ___; *{explosion}*
& Spot the Alpha

13.26.X INVENT A BEGINNING ___
TO STOP AN ENDED ___;
{explosion} & Spot the Alpha

PLATFORM #14

[*This is a Platform long-form. It uses an "explosion" as its implanting-gimmick. The Implant is meant to incite/reinforce compulsive creation of spiritual machinery—in this case a "picture machine" or "picture-making machine" (although this template-pattern could also apply to other spiritual machinery). The "command-lines" follow a pattern, which we could have presented as a short-form formula to save printed space. But, this pattern causes many phrases (or verb uses) to not make sense in the traditional way—which means an item-line may not even "read" immediately. Once a Seeker gets a sense of its basic meaning (rather than protesting its wording), it will register on a Meter. Say the "command-item" out loud, and spot the Alpha-Spirit; then say the "command-item" while spotting the Alpha-Spirit. Perform this in whatever way produces the best "reads" for each item-line until that same action gives "no-reads" three consecutive times.*]

14.0.1 *{spot an explosion}*; *&A*

14.1.1 YOU MUST CONSTRUCT A PICTURE MACHINE; *&A*

14.1.2 YOU MUST NOT CONSTRUCT A PICTURE MACHINE; *& Spot the Alpha*

14.1.3 YOU MUST CONSTRUCT A PICTURE MACHINE, YOU MUST NOT CONSTRUCT A PICTURE MACHINE; *&A*

14.1.4 YOU MUST ERADICATE A PICTURE MACHINE; *&A*

14.1.5 YOU MUST NOT ERADICATE A PICTURE MACHINE; *&A*

14.1.6 YOU MUST ERADICATE A PICTURE MACHINE, YOU MUST NOT ERADICATE A PICTURE MACHINE; *&A*

14.2.1 YOU MUST CREATE A PICTURE MACHINE; *&A*

14.2.2 YOU MUST NOT CREATE A PICTURE MACHINE; *&A*

14.2.3 YOU MUST CREATE A PICTURE MACHINE, YOU MUST NOT CREATE A PICTURE MACHINE; *&A*

14.2.4 YOU MUST DESTROY A PICTURE MACHINE; *&A*

14.2.5 YOU MUST NOT DESTROY A PICTURE MACHINE; *&A*

14.2.6 YOU MUST DESTROY A PICTURE MACHINE, YOU MUST NOT DESTROY A PICTURE MACHINE; *&A*

14.3.1 YOU MUST FEED A PICTURE MACHINE; *& Spot the Alpha*

14.3.2 YOU MUST NOT FEED A PICTURE MACHINE; *&A*

14.3.3 YOU MUST FEED A PICTURE MACHINE, YOU MUST NOT FEED A PICTURE MACHINE; *& Spot the Alpha*

14.3.4 YOU MUST STARVE A PICTURE MACHINE; *&A*

14.3.5 YOU MUST NOT STARVE A PICTURE MACHINE; *&A*

14.3.6 YOU MUST STARVE A PICTURE MACHINE, YOU MUST NOT STARVE A PICTURE MACHINE; *&A*

14.4.1 YOU MUST BELIEVE A PICTURE MACHINE; *&A*

14.4.2 YOU MUST NOT BELIEVE A PICTURE MACHINE; *&A*

14.4.3 YOU MUST BELIEVE A PICTURE MACHINE, YOU MUST NOT BELIEVE A PICTURE MACHINE; *&A*

14.4.4 YOU MUST DISBELIEVE A PICTURE MACHINE; *&A*

14.4.5 YOU MUST NOT DISBELIEVE A PICTURE MACHINE; *& Spot the Alpha*

14.4.6 YOU MUST DISBELIEVE A PICTURE MACHINE, YOU MUST NOT DISBELIEVE A PICTURE MACHINE; *&A*

14.5.1 YOU MUST DESIRE A PICTURE MACHINE; *&A*

14.5.2 YOU MUST NOT DESIRE A PICTURE MACHINE; *&A*

14.5.3 YOU MUST DESIRE A PICTURE MACHINE, YOU MUST NOT DESIRE A PICTURE MACHINE; *&A*

14.5.4 YOU MUST SHUN A PICTURE MACHINE; *&A*

14.5.5 YOU MUST NOT SHUN A PICTURE MACHINE; *&A*

14.5.6 YOU MUST SHUN A PICTURE MACHINE, YOU MUST NOT SHUN A PICTURE MACHINE; *&A*

14.6.1 YOU MUST APPROACH A PICTURE MACHINE; *&A*

14.6.2 YOU MUST NOT APPROACH A PICTURE MACHINE; *&A*

14.6.3 YOU MUST APPROACH A PICTURE MACHINE, YOU MUST NOT APPROACH A PICTURE MACHINE; *&A*

14.6.4 YOU MUST AVOID A PICTURE MACHINE; *&A*

14.6.5 YOU MUST NOT AVOID A PICTURE MACHINE; *&A*

14.6.6 YOU MUST AVOID A PICTURE MACHINE, YOU MUST NOT AVOID A PICTURE MACHINE; *&A*

14.7.1 YOU MUST JOIN A PICTURE MACHINE; *& Spot the Alpha*

14.7.2 YOU MUST NOT JOIN A PICTURE MACHINE; *&A*

14.7.3 YOU MUST JOIN A PICTURE MACHINE, YOU MUST NOT JOIN A PICTURE MACHINE; *& Spot the Alpha*

14.7.4 YOU MUST SEVER A PICTURE MACHINE; *&A*

14.7.5 YOU MUST NOT SEVER A PICTURE MACHINE; *&A*

14.7.6 YOU MUST SEVER A PICTURE MACHINE, YOU MUST NOT SEVER A PICTURE MACHINE; *&A*

14.8.1 YOU MUST CONTACT A PICTURE MACHINE; *&A*

14.8.2 YOU MUST NOT CONTACT A PICTURE MACHINE; *&A*

14.8.3 YOU MUST CONTACT A PICTURE MACHINE, YOU MUST NOT CONTACT A PICTURE MACHINE; *&A*

14.8.4 YOU MUST SEPARATE A PICTURE MACHINE; *&A*

14.8.5 YOU MUST NOT SEPARATE A PICTURE MACHINE; *&A*

14.8.6 YOU MUST SEPARATE A PICTURE MACHINE, YOU MUST NOT SEPARATE A PICTURE MACHINE; *&A*

14.9.1 YOU MUST CONNECT A PICTURE MACHINE; *&A*

14.9.2 YOU MUST NOT CONNECT A PICTURE MACHINE; *&A*

14.9.3 YOU MUST CONNECT A PICTURE MACHINE, YOU MUST NOT CONNECT A PICTURE MACHINE; *&A*

14.9.4 YOU MUST DISCONNECT A PICTURE MACHINE; *&A*

14.9.5 YOU MUST NOT DISCONNECT A PICTURE MACHINE; *& Spot the Alpha*

14.9.6 YOU MUST DISCONNECT A PICTURE MACHINE, YOU MUST NOT DISCONNECT A PICTURE MACHINE; *&A*

14.10.1 YOU MUST COMMUNICATE WITH A PICTURE MACHINE; *& Spot the Alpha*

14.10.2 YOU MUST NOT COMMUNICATE WITH A PICTURE MACHINE; *&A*

14.10.3 YOU MUST COMMUNICATE WITH A PICTURE MACHINE, YOU MUST NOT COMMUNICATE WITH A PICTURE MACHINE; *&A*

14.10.4 YOU MUST SPURN A PICTURE MACHINE; *&A*

14.10.5 YOU MUST NOT SPURN A PICTURE MACHINE; *&A*

14.10.6 YOU MUST SPURN A
PICTURE MACHINE, YOU
MUST NOT SPURN A
PICTURE MACHINE; *&A*

14.11.1 YOU MUST AGREE WITH A
PICTURE MACHINE; *&A*

14.11.2 YOU MUST NOT AGREE
WITH A PICTURE MACHINE;
& Spot the Alpha

14.11.3 YOU MUST AGREE WITH A
PICTURE MACHINE, YOU
MUST NOT AGREE WITH A
PICTURE MACHINE; *&A*

14.11.4 YOU MUST DISAGREE WITH
A PICTURE MACHINE; *&A*

14.11.5 YOU MUST NOT DISAGREE
WITH A PICTURE MACHINE;
& Spot the Alpha

14.11.6 YOU MUST DISAGREE WITH
A PICTURE MACHINE, YOU
MUST NOT DISAGREE WITH
A PICTURE MACHINE; *&A*

14.12.1 YOU MUST LIKE A PICTURE
MACHINE; *& Spot the Alpha*

14.12.2 YOU MUST NOT LIKE A PICTURE MACHINE; *&A*

14.12.3 YOU MUST LIKE A PICTURE MACHINE, YOU MUST NOT LIKE A PICTURE MACHINE; *& Spot the Alpha*

14.12.4 YOU MUST DISLIKE A PICTURE MACHINE; *&A*

14.12.5 YOU MUST NOT DISLIKE A PICTURE MACHINE; *&A*

14.12.6 YOU MUST DISLIKE A PICTURE MACHINE, YOU MUST NOT DISLIKE A PICTURE MACHINE; *&A*

14.13.1 YOU MUST LOVE A PICTURE MACHINE; *& Spot the Alpha*

14.13.2 YOU MUST NOT LOVE A PICTURE MACHINE; *&A*

14.13.3 YOU MUST LOVE A PICTURE MACHINE, YOU MUST NOT LOVE A PICTURE MACHINE; *& Spot the Alpha*

14.13.4 YOU MUST DESPISE A PICTURE MACHINE; *&A*

14.13.5 YOU MUST NOT DESPISE A
PICTURE MACHINE; *&A*

14.13.6 YOU MUST DESPISE A
PICTURE MACHINE, YOU
MUST NOT DESPISE A
PICTURE MACHINE; *&A*

14.14.1 YOU MUST VALUE A
PICTURE MACHINE; *&A*

14.14.2 YOU MUST NOT VALUE A
PICTURE MACHINE; *&A*

14.14.3 YOU MUST VALUE A
PICTURE MACHINE, YOU
MUST NOT VALUE A
PICTURE MACHINE; *&A*

14.14.4 YOU MUST CONDEMN A
PICTURE MACHINE; *&A*

14.14.5 YOU MUST NOT CONDEMN
A PICTURE MACHINE; *&A*

14.14.6 YOU MUST CONDEMN A
PICTURE MACHINE, YOU
MUST NOT CONDEMN A
PICTURE MACHINE; *&A*

14.15.1 YOU MUST WELCOME A
PICTURE MACHINE; *&A*

14.15.2 YOU MUST NOT WELCOME
A PICTURE MACHINE; *&A*

14.15.3 YOU MUST WELCOME A
PICTURE MACHINE, YOU
MUST NOT WELCOME A
PICTURE MACHINE; *&A*

14.15.4 YOU MUST REFUSE A
PICTURE MACHINE; *&A*

14.15.5 YOU MUST NOT REFUSE A
PICTURE MACHINE; *&A*

14.15.6 YOU MUST REFUSE A
PICTURE MACHINE, YOU
MUST NOT REFUSE A
PICTURE MACHINE; *&A*

14.16.1 YOU MUST CONCENTRATE
ON A PICTURE MACHINE;
& Spot the Alpha

14.16.2 YOU MUST NOT
CONCENTRATE ON A
PICTURE MACHINE; *&A*

14.16.3 YOU MUST CONCENTRATE
ON A PICTURE MACHINE,
YOU MUST NOT
CONCENTRATE ON A
PICTURE MACHINE; *&A*

14.16.4 YOU MUST DISPERSE
FROM A PICTURE MACHINE;
& Spot the Alpha

14.16.5 YOU MUST NOT DISPERSE
FROM A PICTURE MACHINE;
& Spot the Alpha

14.16.6 YOU MUST DISPERSE
FROM A PICTURE MACHINE,
YOU MUST NOT DISPERSE
FROM A PICTURE MACHINE;
& Spot the Alpha

14.17.1 YOU MUST FIXATE ON A
PICTURE MACHINE; *&A*

14.17.2 YOU MUST NOT FIXATE ON
A PICTURE MACHINE; *&A*

14.17.3 YOU MUST FIXATE ON A
PICTURE MACHINE, YOU
MUST NOT FIXATE ON A
PICTURE MACHINE; *&A*

14.17.4 YOU MUST DISASSOCIATE
FROM A PICTURE MACHINE;
& Spot the Alpha

14.17.5 YOU MUST NOT
DISASSOCIATE FROM A
PICTURE MACHINE; *&A*

14.17.6 YOU MUST DISASSOCIATE FROM A PICTURE MACHINE, YOU MUST NOT DISASSOCIATE FROM A PICTURE MACHINE; *&A*

14.18.1 YOU MUST HEED A PICTURE MACHINE; *&A*

14.18.2 YOU MUST NOT HEED A PICTURE MACHINE; *&A*

14.18.3 YOU MUST HEED A PICTURE MACHINE, YOU MUST NOT HEED A PICTURE MACHINE; *&A*

14.18.4 YOU MUST IGNORE A PICTURE MACHINE; *&A*

14.18.5 YOU MUST NOT IGNORE A PICTURE MACHINE; *&A*

14.18.6 YOU MUST IGNORE A PICTURE MACHINE, YOU MUST NOT IGNORE A PICTURE MACHINE; *&A*

14.19.1 YOU MUST DEPEND UPON A PICTURE MACHINE; *&A*

14.19.2 YOU MUST NOT DEPEND UPON A PICTURE MACHINE; *& Spot the Alpha*

14.19.3 YOU MUST DEPEND UPON A PICTURE MACHINE, YOU MUST NOT DEPEND UPON A PICTURE MACHINE; *&A*

14.19.4 YOU MUST BLAME A PICTURE MACHINE; *&A*

14.19.5 YOU MUST NOT BLAME A PICTURE MACHINE; *&A*

14.19.6 YOU MUST BLAME A PICTURE MACHINE, YOU MUST NOT BLAME A PICTURE MACHINE; *&A*

14.20.1 YOU MUST MAINTAIN A PICTURE MACHINE; *&A*

14.20.2 YOU MUST NOT MAINTAIN A PICTURE MACHINE; *&A*

14.20.3 YOU MUST MAINTAIN A PICTURE MACHINE, YOU MUST NOT MAINTAIN A PICTURE MACHINE; *&A*

14.20.4 YOU MUST DAMAGE A PICTURE MACHINE; *&A*

14.20.5 YOU MUST NOT DAMAGE A PICTURE MACHINE; *&A*

14.20.6 YOU MUST DAMAGE A PICTURE MACHINE, YOU MUST NOT DAMAGE A PICTURE MACHINE; *&A*

14.21.1 YOU MUST CARE FOR A PICTURE MACHINE; *&A*

14.21.2 YOU MUST NOT CARE FOR A PICTURE MACHINE; *&A*

14.21.3 YOU MUST CARE FOR A PICTURE MACHINE, YOU MUST NOT CARE FOR A PICTURE MACHINE; *&A*

14.21.4 YOU MUST ABUSE A PICTURE MACHINE; *&A*

14.21.5 YOU MUST NOT ABUSE A PICTURE MACHINE; *&A*

14.21.6 YOU MUST ABUSE A PICTURE MACHINE, YOU MUST NOT ABUSE A PICTURE MACHINE; *&A*

14.22.1 YOU MUST HAVE A PICTURE MACHINE; *& Spot the Alpha*

14.22.2 YOU MUST NOT HAVE A PICTURE MACHINE; *&A*

14.22.3 YOU MUST HAVE A PICTURE MACHINE, YOU MUST NOT HAVE A PICTURE MACHINE; *& Spot the Alpha*

14.22.4 YOU MUST DISCARD A PICTURE MACHINE; *&A*

14.22.5 YOU MUST NOT DISCARD A PICTURE MACHINE; *&A*

14.22.6 YOU MUST DISCARD A PICTURE MACHINE, YOU MUST NOT DISCARD A PICTURE MACHINE; *&A*

14.23.1 YOU MUST OBTAIN A PICTURE MACHINE; *&A*

14.23.2 YOU MUST NOT OBTAIN A PICTURE MACHINE; *&A*

14.23.3 YOU MUST OBTAIN A PICTURE MACHINE, YOU MUST NOT OBTAIN A PICTURE MACHINE; *&A*

14.23.4 YOU MUST REJECT A PICTURE MACHINE; *&A*

14.23.5 YOU MUST NOT REJECT A PICTURE MACHINE; *&A*

14.23.6 YOU MUST REJECT A PICTURE MACHINE, YOU MUST NOT REJECT A PICTURE MACHINE; *&A*

14.24.1 YOU MUST ACQUIRE A PICTURE MACHINE; *&A*

14.24.2 YOU MUST NOT ACQUIRE A PICTURE MACHINE; *&A*

14.24.3 YOU MUST ACQUIRE A PICTURE MACHINE, YOU MUST NOT ACQUIRE A PICTURE MACHINE; *&A*

14.24.4 YOU MUST ABANDON A PICTURE MACHINE; *&A*

14.24.5 YOU MUST NOT ABANDON A PICTURE MACHINE; *&A*

14.24.6 YOU MUST ABANDON A PICTURE MACHINE, YOU MUST NOT ABANDON A PICTURE MACHINE; *&A*

14.25.1 YOU MUST USE A PICTURE MACHINE; *& Spot the Alpha*

14.25.2 YOU MUST NOT USE A PICTURE MACHINE; *&A*

14.25.3 YOU MUST USE A PICTURE MACHINE, YOU MUST NOT USE A PICTURE MACHINE; *& Spot the Alpha*

14.25.4 YOU MUST NEGLECT A PICTURE MACHINE; *&A*

14.25.5 YOU MUST NOT NEGLECT A PICTURE MACHINE; *&A*

14.25.6 YOU MUST NEGLECT A PICTURE MACHINE, YOU MUST NOT NEGLECT A PICTURE MACHINE; *&A*

14.26.1 YOU MUST UTILIZE A PICTURE MACHINE; *&A*

14.26.2 YOU MUST NOT UTILIZE A PICTURE MACHINE; *&A*

14.26.3 YOU MUST UTILIZE A PICTURE MACHINE, YOU MUST NOT UTILIZE A PICTURE MACHINE; *&A*

14.26.4 YOU MUST DISPENSE WITH A PICTURE MACHINE; *&A*

14.26.5 YOU MUST NOT DISPENSE WITH A PICTURE MACHINE; *& Spot the Alpha*

14.26.6 YOU MUST DISPENSE WITH A PICTURE MACHINE, YOU MUST NOT DISPENSE WITH A PICTURE MACHINE; *&A*

14.27.1 YOU MUST VALIDATE A PICTURE MACHINE; *&A*

14.27.2 YOU MUST NOT VALIDATE A PICTURE MACHINE; *&A*

14.27.3 YOU MUST VALIDATE A PICTURE MACHINE, YOU MUST NOT VALIDATE A PICTURE MACHINE; *&A*

14.27.4 YOU MUST INVALIDATE A PICTURE MACHINE; *&A*

14.27.5 YOU MUST NOT INVALIDATE A PICTURE MACHINE; *&A*

14.27.6 YOU MUST INVALIDATE A PICTURE MACHINE, YOU MUST NOT INVALIDATE A PICTURE MACHINE; *&A*

14.28.1 YOU MUST EXAGGERATE A PICTURE MACHINE; *&A*

14.28.2 YOU MUST NOT EXAGGERATE A PICTURE MACHINE; *& Spot the Alpha*

14.28.3 YOU MUST EXAGGERATE A PICTURE MACHINE, YOU MUST NOT EXAGGERATE A PICTURE MACHINE; *&A*

14.28.4 YOU MUST REDUCE A PICTURE MACHINE; *&A*

14.28.5 YOU MUST NOT REDUCE A PICTURE MACHINE; *&A*

14.28.6 YOU MUST REDUCE A PICTURE MACHINE, YOU MUST NOT REDUCE A PICTURE MACHINE; *&A*

14.29.1 YOU MUST BOAST ABOUT A PICTURE MACHINE; *&A*

14.29.2 YOU MUST NOT BOAST ABOUT A PICTURE MACHINE; *& Spot the Alpha*

14.29.3 YOU MUST BOAST ABOUT A PICTURE MACHINE, YOU MUST NOT BOAST ABOUT A PICTURE MACHINE; *&A*

14.29.4 YOU MUST APOLOGIZE FOR A PICTURE MACHINE; *&A*

14.29.5 YOU MUST NOT APOLOGIZE FOR A PICTURE MACHINE; *& Spot the Alpha*

14.29.6 YOU MUST APOLOGIZE FOR A PICTURE MACHINE, YOU MUST NOT APOLOGIZE FOR A PICTURE MACHINE; *&A*

14.30.1 YOU MUST COMPLIMENT A PICTURE MACHINE; *&A*

14.30.2 YOU MUST NOT COMPLIMENT A PICTURE MACHINE; *& Spot the Alpha*

14.30.3 YOU MUST COMPLIMENT A PICTURE MACHINE, YOU MUST NOT COMPLIMENT A PICTURE MACHINE; *&A*

14.30.4 YOU MUST EXCUSE A PICTURE MACHINE; *&A*

14.30.5 YOU MUST NOT EXCUSE A PICTURE MACHINE; *&A*

14.30.6 YOU MUST EXCUSE A
PICTURE MACHINE, YOU
MUST NOT EXCUSE A
PICTURE MACHINE; *&A*

14.31.1 YOU MUST SHOW A
PICTURE MACHINE; *&A*

14.31.2 YOU MUST NOT SHOW A
PICTURE MACHINE; *&A*

14.31.3 YOU MUST SHOW A
PICTURE MACHINE, YOU
MUST NOT SHOW A
PICTURE MACHINE; *&A*

14.31.4 YOU MUST SCREEN A
PICTURE MACHINE; *&A*

14.31.5 YOU MUST NOT SCREEN A
PICTURE MACHINE; *&A*

14.31.6 YOU MUST SCREEN A
PICTURE MACHINE, YOU
MUST NOT SCREEN A
PICTURE MACHINE; *&A*

14.32.1 YOU MUST REVEAL A
PICTURE MACHINE; *&A*

14.32.2 YOU MUST NOT REVEAL A
PICTURE MACHINE; *&A*

14.32.3 YOU MUST REVEAL A PICTURE MACHINE, YOU MUST NOT REVEAL A PICTURE MACHINE; *&A*

14.32.4 YOU MUST HIDE A PICTURE MACHINE; *& Spot the Alpha*

14.32.5 YOU MUST NOT HIDE A PICTURE MACHINE; *&A*

14.32.6 YOU MUST HIDE A PICTURE MACHINE, YOU MUST NOT HIDE A PICTURE MACHINE; *& Spot the Alpha*

14.33.1 YOU MUST RECOGNIZE A PICTURE MACHINE; *&A*

14.33.2 YOU MUST NOT RECOGNIZE A PICTURE MACHINE; *& Spot the Alpha*

14.33.3 YOU MUST RECOGNIZE A PICTURE MACHINE, YOU MUST NOT RECOGNIZE A PICTURE MACHINE; *&A*

14.33.4 YOU MUST BLANK-OUT A PICTURE MACHINE; *&A*

14.33.5 YOU MUST NOT BLANK-OUT A PICTURE MACHINE; *&A*

14.33.6 YOU MUST BLANK-OUT A PICTURE MACHINE, YOU MUST NOT BLANK-OUT A PICTURE MACHINE; *&A*

14.34.1 YOU MUST DISCOVER A PICTURE MACHINE; *&A*

14.34.2 YOU MUST NOT DISCOVER A PICTURE MACHINE; *&A*

14.34.3 YOU MUST DISCOVER A PICTURE MACHINE, YOU MUST NOT DISCOVER A PICTURE MACHINE; *&A*

14.34.4 YOU MUST OVERLOOK A PICTURE MACHINE; *&A*

14.34.5 YOU MUST NOT OVERLOOK A PICTURE MACHINE; *&A*

14.34.6 YOU MUST OVERLOOK A PICTURE MACHINE, YOU MUST NOT OVERLOOK A PICTURE MACHINE; *&A*

14.35.1 YOU MUST REMEMBER A PICTURE MACHINE; *&A*

14.35.2 YOU MUST NOT REMEMBER A PICTURE MACHINE; *&A*

14.35.3 YOU MUST REMEMBER A
PICTURE MACHINE, YOU
MUST NOT REMEMBER A
PICTURE MACHINE; *&A*

14.35.4 YOU MUST FORGET A
PICTURE MACHINE; *&A*

14.35.5 YOU MUST NOT FORGET A
PICTURE MACHINE; *&A*

14.35.6 YOU MUST FORGET A
PICTURE MACHINE, YOU
MUST NOT FORGET A
PICTURE MACHINE; *&A*

14.36.1 *{explosion}*; *& Spot the Alpha*

PLATFORM #15

[*This is a Platform long-form. It reinforces activity of the "Picture Machine" from Platform #14. The "command-lines" follow a pattern, which could be presented as a short-form formula. But, this pattern uses a dichotomy (pair) of opposing adjectives for each step. The first "item-lines" of each step do not appear in the actual incident, and are intended to defragment any charge on the*

194

adjectives (words) themselves before running them as command-items. If an area will not register at all, a Seeker may need to figure a similar adjective that fits their understanding (vocabulary) better. Say the "command-item" out loud, and spot the Alpha-Spirit; then say the "command-item" while spotting the Alpha-Spirit. Perform this in whatever way produces the best "reads" for each item-line until that same action gives "no-reads" three consecutive times.]

15.1.A **NICE.**

15.1.B **NAUGHTY.**

15.1.C **NICE, NAUGHTY.**

15.1.1 **COPYING NICE PICTURES;** *& Spot the Alpha*

15.1.2 **NOT COPYING NICE PICTURES;** *& Spot the Alpha*

15.1.3 **HAVING NICE PICTURES;** *& Spot the Alpha*

15.1.4 **NOT HAVING NICE PICTURES;** *& Spot the Alpha*

15.1.5 **USING NICE PICTURES;** *&A*

197

199

**If "MYSTIFYING" does not register below,
try "UNINTELLIGIBLE."*

PLATFORM #16

[This is a Platform short-form formula. The Implant incites or reinforces the decay of goals by opposition. It contains a series of 18 "command-item" lines. This series (lines 1 through 18) is run on each of 82 different keywords. They are listed/numbered below. A Seeker must know the meaning of each of these keywords, and get three consecutive "no-reads" on each by itself, before processing-out the Implant. The list below may be used for that purpose as 'Step-1'.

A Seeker should also prepare 82 different worksheets from this formula, inserting only one keyword (of the 82) for each worksheet. This generates 1476 different command-items total. Don't analyze its fragmented contents; just defragment it.

All item-lines may not read. If necessary for reads, some alternative verbs are listed with an *asterisk. Only backtrack if three consecutive line-items do not register. When an item-line does not read, simply check to see if anything has been "suppressed," "invalidated," or "protested" on that item. For example: "On 'To Create X', has anything been 'suppressed'," &tc. If there is no-read for all of these checks, continue to the next item. If you get a 'big win', end-session for the day. Since excess charge is taken off all keywords at the beginning, and as more of the formula-pattern is defragmented, item-lines may discharge more easily or even cease to register altogether. If three consecutive Platform keyword-worksheets give no-reads (and are not being "suppressed" &tc.), then Platform #16 is defragmented.]

KEYWORDS: 1) SPACE; 2) MATTER;
3) ENERGY; 4) MASS (*SOLIDITY);

5) NEVER; 6) TIME; 7) MOMENTS
(*INSTANTS); 8) ETERNITY; 9) STILLNESS;
10) MOTION (*VELOCITY); 11) VACUUMS;
12) SOLIDS; 13) VOIDS; 14) UNIVERSES;
15) STARS; 16) GALAXIES; 17) PLANETS;
18) SUNS; 19) SYSTEMS; 20) CLUSTERS;
21) DEADNESS; 22) BRIGHTNESS;
23) DARKNESS; 24) LIGHT;
25) BLACKNESS; 26) WHITENESS;
27) BLUENESS; 28) REDNESS;
29) YELLOWNESS; 30) GREENNESS;
31) PURPLENESS; 32) ORANGENESS;
33) SILENCE; 34) SOUNDS; 35) NOISE;
36) MUSIC; 37) DISHARMONY; 38)
HARMONY; 39) LIQUIDS; 40) GASES;
41) COLD; 42) HEAT; 43) DESERTS;
44) SEAS; 45) VALLEYS; 46) MOUNTAINS;
47) BROOKS; 48) RIVERS; 49) ISLANDS;
50) CONTINENTS; 51) METEORS; 52)
COMETS; 53) VOIDS; 54) HABITATIONS;
55) BARBARISMS; 56) CIVILIZATIONS;
57) ANARCHY; 58) GOVERNMENT;
59) SAVAGES; 60) HUMANS; 61) ANIMALS;
62) PEOPLE; 63) INSECTS; 64) SNAKES;
65) MONSTERS; 66) FISH; 67) CELLS;
68) BODIES; 69) POISONS; 70) BALMS;
71) DEPRESSANTS; 72) STIMULANTS;
73) SEDATIVES; 74) EUPHORICS;
75) ILLUSIONS; 76) REALITIES;
77) DELUSIONS; 78) ACTUALITIES;
79) LIES; 80) TRUTHS; 81) IGNORANCE;
82) KNOWLEDGE.

16.1.X TO CREATE ___; &A

16.2.X NO MORE DESIRES TO CREATE ___; & Spot the Alpha

16.3.X DIFFERENTLY CREATING ___; & Spot the Alpha

16.4.X DIFFICULTIES WITH OTHER CREATORS OF ___; &A

16.5.X CONSTANTLY CREATING ___; & Spot the Alpha

16.6.X FAILURES TO CREATE ___; & Spot the Alpha

16.7.X AUTOMATIC CREATORS OF ___; & Spot the Alpha

16.8.X OBSESSION WITH TO CREATE ___; & Spot the Alpha

16.9.X HAVING TO CREATE ___; &A

16.10.X COMPULSIONS TO CREATE ___; & Spot the Alpha

16.11.X HATING TO CREATE ___; &A

16.12.X CRITICISMS OF CREATED ___; & Spot the Alpha

16.13.X HOPING TO NEVER CREATE ___; & Spot the Alpha

213

16.14.X **TOO MUCH CREATING ___;**
            & Spot the Alpha

16.15.X **TO NEVER CREATE ___;** *&A*

16.16.X **TO CREATE ___;** *&A*

16.17.X **DESIRES TO DESTROY ___;**
            &A

16.18.X **THOSE WHO DESIRE TO CREATE ___;** *& Spot the Alpha*

PLATFORM #17

[This is a Platform long-form. It is meant to incite or reinforce a fixation on bodies. The "command-lines" follow a pattern, which we could have presented as a short-form formula. If an item-line does not "read" immediately, it may be necessary for a Seeker to figure an alternative similar verb. Once a Seeker gets a sense of its basic meaning (rather than protesting its wording), it will register on a Meter. Say the "command-item" out loud, and spot the Alpha-Spirit; then say the "command-item" while spotting the Alpha-Spirit. Perform this in whatever way produces the

best "reads" for each item-line until that same action gives "no-reads" three consecutive times. Remember that you are treating an incident; so you might consider the item-lines as "During {command-item}; Spot the Alpha." ("Spot the Alpha" may be abbreviated as "&A.")]

17.1.1 **TO LOVE A BODY;** *&A*
17.1.2 **TO NOT LOVE A BODY;** *&A*
17.1.3 **TO LOVE A BODY, TO NOT LOVE A BODY;** *&A*
17.1.4 **TO HATE A BODY;** *&A*
17.1.5 **TO NOT HATE A BODY;** *&A*
17.1.6 **TO HATE A BODY, TO NOT HATE A BODY;** *&A*

17.2.1 **TO WANT A BODY;** *&A*
17.2.2 **TO NOT WANT A BODY;** *&A*
17.2.3 **TO WANT A BODY, TO NOT WANT A BODY;** *&A*
17.2.4 **TO PROTEST A BODY;** *&A*
17.2.5 **TO NOT PROTEST A BODY;** *& Spot the Alpha*
17.2.6 **TO PROTEST A BODY, TO NOT PROTEST A BODY;** *&A*

17.3.1   TO ACQUIRE A BODY; *&A*

17.3.2   TO NOT ACQUIRE A BODY;
& Spot the Alpha

17.3.3   TO ACQUIRE A BODY, TO
NOT ACQUIRE A BODY; *&A*

17.3.4   TO REJECT A BODY; *&A*

17.3.5   TO NOT REJECT A BODY;
& Spot the Alpha

17.3.6   TO REJECT A BODY, TO NOT
REJECT A BODY; *&A*

17.4.1   TO NEED A BODY; *&A*

17.4.2   TO NOT NEED A BODY; *&A*

17.4.3   TO NEED A BODY, TO NOT
NEED A BODY; *&A*

17.4.4   TO CONDEMN A BODY; *&A*

17.4.5   TO NOT CONDEMN A BODY;
& Spot the Alpha

17.4.6   TO CONDEMN A BODY, TO
NOT CONDEMN A BODY; *&A*

17.5.1   TO DO WITH A BODY; *&A*

17.5.2   TO NOT DO WITH A BODY;
& Spot the Alpha

17.5.3   TO DO WITH A BODY, TO
NOT DO WITH A BODY; *&A*

17.5.4 TO DO WITHOUT A BODY;
& Spot the Alpha

17.5.5 TO NOT DO WITHOUT A
BODY; *& Spot the Alpha*

17.5.6 TO DO WITHOUT A BODY,
TO NOT DO WITHOUT A
BODY; *& Spot the Alpha*

17.6.1 TO HAVE A BODY; *&A*

17.6.2 TO NOT HAVE A BODY; *&A*

17.6.3 TO HAVE A BODY, TO NOT
HAVE A BODY; *&A*

17.6.4 TO GET RID OF A BODY; *&A*

17.6.5 TO NOT GET RID OF A
BODY; *& Spot the Alpha*

17.6.6 TO GET RID OF A BODY, TO
NOT GET RID OF A BODY;
& Spot the Alpha

17.7.1 TO SEEK A BODY; *&A*

17.7.2 TO NOT SEEK A BODY; *&A*

17.7.3 TO SEEK A BODY, TO NOT
SEEK A BODY; *&A*

17.7.4 TO FORGET A BODY; *&A*

17.7.5 TO NOT FORGET A BODY;
& Spot the Alpha

17.15.3 TO SHOW A BODY, TO NOT SHOW A BODY; *&A*

17.15.4 TO CURTAIN A BODY; *&A*

17.15.5 TO NOT CURTAIN A BODY; *& Spot the Alpha*

17.15.6 TO CURTAIN A BODY, TO NOT CURTAIN A BODY; *&A*

17.16.1 TO APPEAR IN A BODY; *&A*

17.16.2 TO NOT APPEAR IN A BODY; *& Spot the Alpha*

17.16.3 TO APPEAR IN A BODY, TO NOT APPEAR IN A BODY; *& Spot the Alpha*

17.16.4 TO DISAPPEAR IN A BODY; *& Spot the Alpha*

17.16.5 TO NOT DISAPPEAR IN A BODY; *& Spot the Alpha*

17.16.6 TO DISAPPEAR IN A BODY, TO NOT DISAPPEAR IN A BODY; *& Spot the Alpha*

17.17.1 TO BE A BODY; *&A*

17.17.2 TO NOT BE A BODY; *&A*

17.17.3 TO BE A BODY, TO NOT BE A BODY; *& Spot the Alpha*

17.17.4 TO UN-BE A BODY; *&A*

17.17.5 TO NOT UN-BE A BODY; *&A*

17.17.6 TO UN-BE A BODY, TO NOT UN-BE A BODY; *&A*

17.18.1 TO FLAUNT A BODY; *&A*

17.18.2 TO NOT FLAUNT A BODY; *& Spot the Alpha*

17.18.3 TO FLAUNT A BODY, TO NOT FLAUNT A BODY; *&A*

17.18.4 TO CONCEAL A BODY; *&A*

17.18.5 TO NOT CONCEAL A BODY; *& Spot the Alpha*

17.18.6 TO CONCEAL A BODY, TO NOT CONCEAL A BODY; *&A*

17.19.1 TO DEMONSTRATE A BODY; *& Spot the Alpha*

17.19.2 TO NOT DEMONSTRATE A BODY; *& Spot the Alpha*

17.19.3 TO DEMONSTRATE A BODY, TO NOT DEMONSTRATE A BODY; *& Spot the Alpha*

17.19.4 TO COVER A BODY; *&A*

17.19.5 TO NOT COVER A BODY; *&A*

17.19.6 TO COVER A BODY, TO NOT
COVER A BODY; *&A*

17.20.1 TO BEAUTIFY A BODY; *&A*

17.20.2 TO NOT BEAUTIFY A BODY;
& Spot the Alpha

17.20.3 TO BEAUTIFY A BODY, TO
NOT BEAUTIFY A BODY; *&A*

17.20.4 TO UGLIFY A BODY; *&A*

17.20.5 TO NOT UGLIFY A BODY; *&A*

17.20.6 TO UGLIFY A BODY, TO NOT
UGLIFY A BODY; *&A*

17.21.1 TO ENNOBLE A BODY; *&A*

17.21.2 TO NOT ENNOBLE A BODY;
& Spot the Alpha

17.21.3 TO ENNOBLE A BODY, TO
NOT ENNOBLE A BODY; *&A*

17.21.4 TO DEGRADE A BODY; *&A*

17.21.5 TO NOT DEGRADE A BODY;
& Spot the Alpha

17.21.6 TO DEGRADE A BODY, TO
NOT DEGRADE A BODY; *&A*

17.22.1 TO PROMOTE A BODY; *&A*

17.22.2 TO NOT PROMOTE A BODY;
& Spot the Alpha

17.24.6 TO HINDER A BODY, TO NOT HINDER A BODY; *&A*

17.25.1 TO SAVE A BODY; *&A*

17.25.2 TO NOT SAVE A BODY; *&A*

17.25.3 TO SAVE A BODY, TO NOT SAVE A BODY; *&A*

17.25.4 TO WASTE A BODY; *&A*

17.25.5 TO NOT WASTE A BODY; *&A*

17.25.6 TO WASTE A BODY, TO NOT WASTE A BODY; *&A*

17.26.1 TO PRESERVE A BODY; *&A*

17.26.2 TO NOT PRESERVE A BODY; *& Spot the Alpha*

17.26.3 TO PRESERVE A BODY, TO NOT PRESERVE A BODY; *& Spot the Alpha*

17.26.4 TO DECAY A BODY; *&A*

17.26.5 TO NOT DECAY A BODY; *&A*

17.26.6 TO DECAY A BODY, TO NOT DECAY A BODY; *&A*

17.27.1 TO STIMULATE A BODY; *&A*

17.27.2 TO NOT STIMULATE A BODY; *& Spot the Alpha*

17.27.3 TO STIMULATE A BODY, TO NOT STIMULATE A BODY; *& Spot the Alpha*

17.27.4 TO DESTIMULATE A BODY; *& Spot the Alpha*

17.27.5 TO NOT DESTIMULATE A BODY; *& Spot the Alpha*

17.27.6 TO DESTIMULATE A BODY, TO NOT DESTIMULATE A BODY; *& Spot the Alpha*

17.28.1 TO PROTECT A BODY; *&A*

17.28.2 TO NOT PROTECT A BODY; *& Spot the Alpha*

17.28.3 TO PROTECT A BODY, TO NOT PROTECT A BODY; *&A*

17.28.4 TO HARM A BODY; *&A*

17.28.5 TO NOT HARM A BODY; *&A*

17.28.6 TO HARM A BODY, TO NOT HARM A BODY; *&A*

17.29.1 TO DEFEND A BODY; *&A*

17.29.2 TO NOT DEFEND A BODY; *& Spot the Alpha*

17.29.3 TO DEFEND A BODY, TO NOT DEFEND A BODY; *&A*

17.29.4   TO ATTACK A BODY; *&A*

17.29.5   TO NOT ATTACK A BODY;
& Spot the Alpha

17.29.6   TO ATTACK A BODY, TO NOT ATTACK A BODY; *&A*

17.30.1   TO ENERGIZE A BODY; *&A*

17.30.2   TO NOT ENERGIZE A BODY;
& Spot the Alpha

17.30.3   TO ENERGIZE A BODY, TO NOT ENERGIZE A BODY; *&A*

17.30.4   TO DE-ENERGIZE A BODY;
& Spot the Alpha

17.30.5   TO NOT DE-ENERGIZE A BODY; *& Spot the Alpha*

17.30.6   TO DE-ENERGIZE A BODY, TO NOT DE-ENERGIZE A BODY; *& Spot the Alpha*

17.31.1   TO ENTHUSE A BODY; *&A*

17.31.2   TO NOT ENTHUSE A BODY;
& Spot the Alpha

17.31.3   TO ENTHUSE A BODY, TO NOT ENTHUSE A BODY; *&A*

17.31.4   TO SUPPRESS A BODY; *&A*

17.31.5 **TO NOT SUPPRESS A BODY;**
& Spot the Alpha

17.31.6 **TO SUPPRESS A BODY, TO NOT SUPPRESS A BODY;**
& Spot the Alpha

17.32.1 **TO ELEVATE A BODY;** *&A*

17.32.2 **TO NOT ELEVATE A BODY;**
& Spot the Alpha

17.32.3 **TO ELEVATE A BODY, TO NOT ELEVATE A BODY;** *&A*

17.32.4 **TO DEPRESS A BODY;** *&A*

17.32.5 **TO NOT DEPRESS A BODY;**
& Spot the Alpha

17.32.6 **TO DEPRESS A BODY, TO NOT DEPRESS A BODY;** *&A*

17.33.1 **TO ENHANCE A BODY;** *&A*

17.33.2 **TO NOT ENHANCE A BODY;**
& Spot the Alpha

17.33.3 **TO ENHANCE A BODY, TO NOT ENHANCE A BODY;** *&A*

17.33.4 **TO DISPARAGE A BODY;** *&A*

17.33.5 **TO NOT DISPARAGE A BODY;** *& Spot the Alpha*

17.33.6 TO DISPARAGE A BODY, TO NOT DISPARAGE A BODY; *& Spot the Alpha*

17.34.1 TO GLORIFY A BODY; *&A*

17.34.2 TO NOT GLORIFY A BODY; *& Spot the Alpha*

17.34.3 TO GLORIFY A BODY, TO NOT GLORIFY A BODY; *&A*

17.34.4 TO BELITTLE A BODY; *&A*

17.34.5 TO NOT BELITTLE A BODY; *& Spot the Alpha*

17.34.6 TO BELITTLE A BODY, TO NOT BELITTLE A BODY; *&A*

17.35.1 TO EXPAND A BODY; *&A*

17.35.2 TO NOT EXPAND A BODY; *& Spot the Alpha*

17.35.3 TO EXPAND A BODY, TO NOT EXPAND A BODY; *&A*

17.35.4 TO CONTRACT A BODY; *&A*

17.35.5 TO NOT CONTRACT A BODY; *& Spot the Alpha*

17.35.6 TO CONTRACT A BODY, TO NOT CONTRACT A BODY; *& Spot the Alpha*

17.36.1 TO EXERCISE A BODY; *&A*

17.36.2 TO NOT EXERCISE A BODY; *& Spot the Alpha*

17.36.3 TO EXERCISE A BODY, TO NOT EXERCISE A BODY; *&A*

17.36.4 TO RELAX A BODY; *&A*

17.36.5 TO NOT RELAX A BODY; *&A*

17.36.6 TO RELAX A BODY, TO NOT RELAX A BODY; *&A*

17.37.1 TO USE A BODY; *&A*

17.37.2 TO NOT USE A BODY; *&A*

17.37.3 TO USE A BODY, TO NOT USE A BODY; *& Spot the Alpha*

17.37.4 TO DISUSE A BODY; *&A*

17.37.5 TO NOT DISUSE A BODY; *& Spot the Alpha*

17.37.6 TO DISUSE A BODY, TO NOT DISUSE A BODY; *&A*

17.38.1 TO BEGIN A BODY; *&A*

17.38.2 TO NOT BEGIN A BODY; *&A*

17.38.3 TO BEGIN A BODY, TO NOT BEGIN A BODY; *&A*

17.38.4 TO END A BODY; *&A*

17.38.5 TO NOT END A BODY; *&A*

17.38.6 TO END A BODY, TO NOT END A BODY; *& Spot the Alpha*

PLATFORM #18

[*This is a Platform short-form formula. It incites or reinforces the creation of 96 types of spiritual machinery (and unknowingly shifting responsibility), using 96 different conceptual keywords. The first 48 are positives (or constructive/creative); the second 48 are directly oppositional to the first 48. The same formula-pattern of only three command-lines is applied to each of the 96 concepts/words (generating 288 item-lines total). The words are listed/numbered below. A Seeker must know the meaning of each, and get three consecutive "no-reads" on each by itself, before handling the Implant. The list below may be used for that purpose as 'Step-1'.*

A Seeker does not need separate worksheets for each of the 96 types. This is all part of one Platform, using the same pattern of three command-lines 96 times.

All item-lines may not read. When a line does not read, check if anything has been "suppressed," "invalidated," or "protested" about that item. This is important because most of this Platform utilizes non-traditional conceptual wording.

For example: when referring to 'the machine' part, an "–ingness" is added to the end of the keyword (verb). "To Write" (not actually in the list) would be applied as "To Build a Writingness Machine"; and the second line would be "Not 'To Write' Yourself." Most item-lines will appear much less grammatically correct than even this. Remember that this Platform was not Implanted in "English" or any human speech, so we must be somewhat creative in its proper handling.]

KEYWORDS {POSITIVE}: 1) TO POSTULATE; 2) TO THINK; 3) TO IDEA-IZE; 4) TO REASON; 5) TO SOLVE; 6) TO ORDER; 7) TO SPACE; 8) TO TIME; 9) TO MASS; 10) TO ENERGIZE; 11) TO MATERIALIZE; 12) TO SOLIDIFY; 13) TO FIND; 14) TO LOCATE; 15) TO POSITION; 16) TO WANT;

17) TO DESIRE; 18) TO CRAVE; 19) TO GET; 20) TO OBTAIN; 21) TO COLLECT; 22) TO RETAIN; 23) TO KEEP; 24) TO HOLD; 25) TO SAVE; 26) TO PRESERVE; 27) TO SURVIVE; 28) TO RECORD; 29) TO COPY; 30) TO DUPLICATE; 31) TO FORM; 32) TO PICTURE; 33) TO CREATE; 34) TO MAKE; 35) TO PRODUCE; 36) TO CONSTRUCT; 37) TO VIEW; 38) TO SEE; 39) TO PERCEIVE; 40) TO SENSE; 41) TO FEEL; 42) TO CONTACT; 43) TO SENSATION; 44) TO ENJOY; 45) TO EXALT; 46) TO REMEMBER; 47) TO CONSCIOUS-IZE; 48) TO KNOW.

KEYWORDS {NEGATING}: 49) TO WITHHOLD; 50) TO UNTHINKIFY; 51) TO STUPIDIFY; 52) TO UNREASONIZE; 53) TO PROBLEMIFY; 54) TO CONFUSE; 55) TO GROUP; 56) TO TIMELESS; 57) TO CLEAR; 58) TO DRAIN; 59) TO VANISH; 60) TO DISINTEGRATE; 61) TO LOSE; 62) TO HIDE; 63) TO DISPLACE; 64) TO REJECT; 65) TO DISDAIN; 66) TO HATE; 67) TO DISCARD; 68) TO NEGLECT; 69) TO ABANDON; 70) TO IGNORE; 71) TO DISMISS; 72) TO FREE; 73) TO WASTE; 74) TO DECAY; 75) TO DIE; 76) TO ERADICATE; 77) TO ERASE; 78) TO ANNIHILATE; 79) TO TERMINATE; 80) TO BLANK; 81) TO DESTROY; 82) TO IMPEDE; 83) TO STOP; 84) TO ABOLISH; ...

85) TO OBSCURE; 86) TO BLIND; 87) TO SCREEN; 88) TO AVOID; 89) TO SHUN; 90) TO DISCONNECT; 91) TO NUMB; 92) TO SUPPRESS; 93) TO SUBDUE; 94) TO FORGET; 95) TO UNCONSCIOUS-IZE; 96) TO AMNESIA-IZE.

18.X.1 TO BUILD A ___-INGNESS MACHINE; *& Spot the Alpha*

18.X.2 NOT TO ___ YOURSELF; *& Spot the Alpha*

18.X.3 TO BUILD A ___-INGNESS MACHINE, NOT TO ___ YOURSELF; *& Spot the Alpha*

Upon successful *defragmentation* of *Platform #18*, a *Seeker* reaches the next stable-point on the *Pathway*. As a *processing gradient*, this achievement marks the completion of *Systemology Level-7*. Following the standard organizational structure of our *Systemology Society*, a *Seeker* is now "awarded" their own *Implanted Universe Directory* (*AT Manual #4*) prior to approaching *Systemology Level-8* (with *AT Manual #5*).

Congratulations, *Seeker*.

You are further than you might think.

Your next Advanced Training manual is:
"Implanted Universes"

BASIC SYSTEMOLOGY GLOSSARY

actualization : to make actual, not just potential; to bring into full solid Reality; to realize fully in *Awareness* as a "thing."

agreement (reality) : unanimity of opinion of what is "thought" to be known; an accepted arrangement of how things are; things we consider as "real" or as an "is" of "reality"; a consensus of what is real as made by standard-issue (common) participants; what an individual contributes to or accepts as "real"; in *Systemology*, a synonym for "*reality.*"

alpha : the first, primary, basic, superior or beginning of some form; in *Systemology*, referring to the state of existence operating on spiritual archetypes and postulates, will and intention "exterior" to the low-level condensation and solidarity of energy and matter as the 'physical universe' (*beta*).

alpha-spirit : a "spiritual" *Life*-form; the "true" *Self* or I-AM; the *individual*; the spiritual (*alpha*) *Self* that is animating the (*beta*) physical body or "*genetic vehicle*" using a continuous *Lifeline* of spiritual ("*ZU*") energy; an individual spiritual (*alpha*) entity possessing no physical mass or measurable waveform (motion) in the Physical Universe as itself, so it animates the (*beta*) physical body or "*genetic vehicle*" as a catalyst to experience *Self*-determined causality in effect within the *Physical Universe*; a singular unit or point of *Spiritual Awareness* that is *Aware* that it is *Aware*.

alpha thought : the highest spiritual *Self-determination* over creation and existence exercised by an Alpha-Spirit; the Alpha range of pure *Creative Ability* based on direct postulates and considerations of *Beingness*; spiritual qualities comparable to "thought" but originating in Alpha-existence, independently superior to a Mind-System.

ascension : actualized *Awareness* elevated to the point of true "spiritual existence" exterior to *beta existence*. An "Ascended Master" is one who has returned to an incarnation on Earth as an inherently *Enlightened One*, demonstrable in their words and actions; they have the ability to *Self-direct* the "Mind" and "Body" as *Self* (as a "Spirit"); and to maintain consciousness as a personal identity continuum with the same *Self-directed* control and communication of Will-Intention that is exercised, actualized and developed deliberately during one's present incarnation.

associative knowledge : significance or meaning of a facet or aspect assigned to (or considered to have) a direct relationship with another facet; to connect or relate ideas or facets of existence with one another; in traditional systems logic, an equivalency of significance or meaning between facets or sets that are grouped together, such as in $(a + b) + c = a + (b + c)$; in Systemology, erroneous associative knowledge is assignment of the same value to all facets or parts considered as related (even when they are not actually so), such as in $a = a, b = a, c = a$ and so forth without distinction.

attention : active use of *Awareness* toward a specific aspect or thing; the act of "attending" with the presence of *Self*; a direction of focus or concentration of *Awareness* along a particular channel or conduit or toward a particular terminal node or communication termination point; the Self-directed concentration of personal energy as a combination of observation, thought-waves and consideration; focused application of *Self-Directed Awareness*.

awareness : the highest sense of-and-as *Self* in knowing and being as I-AM (the *Alpha-Spirit*); the extent of beingness directed as a viewpoint (POV) experienced by *Self* as *Knowingness*.

beta (awareness) : all consciousness activity ("*Awareness*") in the "Physical Universe" (KI, in *Zuism*) or else in *beta-existence*; *Awareness* within the range of the *genetic-body*, including material thoughts, emotional responses and physical motors; personal *Awareness* of physical energy and physical matter moving through physical space and experienced as "time"; the *Awareness* held by *Self* that is restricted to an organic *Lifeform* or "*genetic vehicle*" in which it experiences causality in *beta-existence*.

beta (existence) : all manifestation in the "Physical Universe" (KI, in *Zuism*); the conditions of *Awareness* for the *Alpha-spirit* (*Self*) as a physical organic *Lifeform* or "*genetic vehicle*" in which it experiences causality in the *Physical Universe*.

charge : to fill or furnish with a quality; to supply with energy; to lay a command upon; in *Systemology*—to imbue with intention; to overspread with emotion; personal energy stores and significances entwined as fragmentation in mental images, reactive-response encoding and intellectual (and/or) programmed beliefs.

channel : a specific stream, course, current, direction or route; to form or cut a groove or ridge or otherwise guide along a specific course; a direct path; an artificial aqueduct created to connect two water bodies or water or make travel possible.

circuit : a circular path or loop; a closed-path within a system that allows a flow; a pattern or action or wave movement that follows a specific route or potential path only; in *Systemology,* "*communication processing*" pertaining to a specific *flow* of energy or information along a channel; "*feedback loop.*"

communication : successful transmission of information, data, energy (&tc.) along a message line, with a reception of feedback; an energetic flow of intention to cause an effect (or duplication) at a distance; the personal energy moved or acted upon by will or else 'selective directed attention'; the 'messenger action' used to transmit and receive energy across a medium; also relay of energy, a message or signal—or even locating a personal POV (viewpoint) for the Self—along the *ZU-line*.

condense (condensation) : the transition of vapor to liquid; denoting a change in state to a more substantial or solid condition; leading to a more compact or solid form.

confront : to come around in front of; to be in the presence of; to stand in front of, or in the face of; to meet "face-to-face" or "face-up-to"; additionally, in *Systemology,* to fully tolerate or acceptably withstand an encounter with a particular manifestation without an automatic reactive response.

240

consideration : careful analytical reflection of all aspects; deliberation; determining the significance of a "thing" in relation to similarity or dissimilarity to other "things"; evaluation of facts and importance of certain facts; thorough examination of all aspects related to, or important for, making a decision; the analysis of consequences and estimation of significance when making decisions; also in *Systemology*, the *postulate* or *Alpha-Thought* that defines the state of *beingness* for what something "*is.*"

defragmentation : the *reparation* of wholeness; collecting all dispersed parts to reform an original whole; a process of removing "*fragmentation*" in data or knowledge to provide a clear understanding; applying techniques and processes that promote a *holistic* interconnected *alpha* state, favoring observational *Awareness* of continuity in all spiritual and physical systems; in *Systemology*, a "*Seeker*" achieving actualized "*Self-Honest Awareness*" is said to be in a basic state of *beta-defragmentation*, whereas *Alpha-defragmentation* is the rehabilitation of the *creative ability*, managing the *Spiritual Timeline* and the POV of *Self* as Alpha-Spirit (I-AM).

existence : the *state* or fact of *apparent manifestation*; the resulting combination of the Principles of Manifestation: consciousness, motion and substance; continued *survival*; that which independently exists.

exterior : outside of; on the outside; in *Systemology*, we mean specifically the POV of *Self* that is *'outside of'* the *Human Condition,* free of the physical and mental trappings of the Physical Universe; a metahuman range of consideration; see also '*Zu-Vision*'.

external : a force coming from outside; information received from outside sources; in *Systemology*, the objective *'Physical Universe'* existence, or *beta-existence*, that the Physical Body or *genetic vehicle* is essentially *anchored* to for its considerations of locational space-time as a dimension or POV.

fragmentation : breaking into parts and scattering the pieces; the *fractioning* of wholeness or the *fracture* of a holistic interconnected *alpha* state, favoring observational *Awareness* of perceived connectivity between parts; *discontinuity*; separation of a totality into parts; in *Systemology*, a person outside of *Self-Honesty* is said to be operating from a *fragmented* state.

flow : movement across (or through) a channel (or conduit); a direction of active energetic motion, typically distinguished as either an *in-flow*, *out-flow* or *cross-flow*.

genetic-vehicle : a physical *Life*-form; the physical (*beta*) body that is animated/controlled by the (*Alpha*) *Spirit* using a continuous *Spiritual Lifeline* (ZU); a physical (*beta*) organic receptacle and catalyst for the (*Alpha*) *Self* to operate "causes" and experience "effects" within the *Physical Universe*.

harmful-act : a counter-survival mode of behavior or action (esp. that causes harm to one of more *Spheres of Existence*)—or—an overtly aggressive (hostile and/or destructive) action against an individual or any other *Sphere of Existence*; in *Utilitarian Systemology*—a shortsighted (serves fewest/lowest *Spheres of Existence*) intentional overtly harmful action to resolve a perceived problem; a revision of the rule for standard *Utilitarianism* for Systemology to distinguish actions which provide the least benefit to the least number of *Spheres of Existence*, or else the greatest harm to the greatest number of *Spheres of Existence*; in *moral philosophy*—an action which can be experienced by few and/or which one would not be willing to experience for themselves (*theft, slander, rape, &tc*); an iniquity or iniquitous act.

hold-back : withheld communications (esp. actions) such as "*Hold-Outs*"; intentional (or automatic) withdrawal (as opposed to reach); Self-restraint (which may eventually be enforced or automated); not reaching, acting or expressing, when one should be; an ability that is now restrained (on automatic) due to inability to withhold it on Self-determinism alone.

hold-outs : in photography, the numerous snapshots/pictures withheld from the final display or professional presentation of the event; withheld communications; in Utilitarian Systemology—energetic withdrawal and communication breaks with a "*terminal*" and its *Sphere of Existence* as a result of a "*Harmful-Act*"; unspoken or undiscovered (hidden, covert) actions that an individual withholds communications of, fearing punishment or endangerment of *Self-preservation* (*First Sphere*); the act of hiding (or keeping hidden) the truth of a "*Harmful-Act*"; a refusal to communicate with a *Pilot*; also "*Hold-Back.*"

holistic : the examination of interconnected systems as encompassing something greater than the *sum* of their "parts."

Human Condition : a standard default state of Human experience that is generally accepted to be the extent of its potential identity (*beingness*) —currently treated as *Homo Sapiens Sapiens,* but which is scheduled for replacement by *Homo Novus* (the "New Human").

imagination : ability to create *mental imagery* in one's Personal Universe at will and change or alter it as desired; the ability to create, change and dissolve mental images on command or as an act of will; to create a mental image or have associated imagery displayed (or "conjured") in the mind that may or may not be treated as real (or memory recall) and may or may not accurately duplicate objective reality; to employ *creative abilities* of the Spirit that are independent of reality agreements with beta-existence.

imprint : to strongly impress, stamp, mark (or outline) onto a softer 'impressible' substance; to mark with pressure onto a surface; in *Systemology*, used to indicate permanent Reality impressions marked by frequencies, energies or interactions experienced during periods of emotional distress, pain, unconsciousness, loss, enforcement, or something antagonistic to physical (personal) survival, all of which are are stored with other reactive response-mechanisms at lower-levels of *Awareness* as opposed to the active memory database and proactive processing center of the Mind; an experiential "memory-set" that may later resurface—be triggered or stimulated artificially—as Reality, of which similar responses will be engaged automatically; holographic-like imagery "stamped" onto consciousness as composed of energetic *facets* tied to the "snap-shot" of an experience.

imprinting incident : the first or original event

instance communicated and *emotionally encoded* onto an individual's "*Spiritual Timeline*" (recorded memory from all lifetimes), which formed a permanent impression that is later used to mechanistically treat future contact on that channel; the first or original occurrence of some particular *facet* or mental image related to a certain type of *encoded response*, such as pain and discomfort, losses and victimization, and even the acts that we have taken against others along the *Spiritual Timeline* of our existence that caused them to also be *Imprinted*.

intention : directed application of Will; to intend (have "in Mind") or signify (give "significance" to) for or toward a particular purpose; in *Systemology* (from the *Standard Model*)—the spiritual activity at WILL (5.0) directed by an *Alpha Spirit* (7.0); the application of WILL as "Cause" from a higher order of Alpha Thought and consideration (6.0).

interior : inside of; on the inside; in *Systemology*, we mean specifically the POV of *Self* that is fixed to the *'internal' Human Condition,* including the *Reactive Control Center* (RCC) and Mind-System or *Master Control Center* (MCC); within *beta-existence*.

internal : a force coming from inside; information received from inside sources; in *Systemology*, the objective experience of *beta-existence* associated with the Physical Body or *genetic vehicle* and its POV regarding sensation and perception; from inside the body; in the body.

invalidate : decrease the level or degree or *agreement* as Reality.

mental image : a subjectively experienced "picture" created and imagined into being by the Alpha-Spirit (or at lower levels, one of its automated mechanisms) that includes all perceptible *facets* of totally immersive scene, which may be forms originated by an individual, or a "facsimile-copy" ("snap-shot") of something seen or encountered; a duplication of wave-forms in one's Personal Universe as a "picture" that mirror an "external" Universe experience, such as an *Imprint*.

perception : internalized processing of data received by the *senses*; to become *Aware of* via the senses.

pilot : a professional steersman responsible for healthy functional operation of a ship toward a specific destination; in *Systemology*, an intensive trained individual qualified to specially apply *Systemology Processing* to assist other *Seekers* on the *Pathway*.

point-of-view (POV) : a point to view from; an opinion or attitude as expressed from a specific identity-phase; a specific standpoint or vantage-point; a definitive manner of consideration specific to an individual phase or identity; a place or position affording a specific view or vantage; circumstances and programming of an individual that is conducive to a particular response, consideration or belief-set (paradigm); a position (consideration) or place (location) that provides a specific view or perspective (subjective) on experience (of the objective).

postulate : to put forward as truth; to suggest or assume an existence *to be*; to state or affirm the existence of particular conditions; to provide a basis of reasoning and belief; a basic theory accepted as fact; in *Systemology*, Alpha-Thought —the top-most decisions or considerations made by the Alpha-Spirit regarding the "*isness*" (what things "are") about energy-matter and space-time.

presence : a quality of some thing (*energy/matter*) being "present" in space-time; personal orientation of *Self* as an *Awareness* (*POV*) located in present space-time (environment) and communicating with extant energy-matter.

processing command line (PCL) : a directed input; a specific command using highly selective language for *Systemology Processing*; a predetermined directive statement (cause) intended to focus concentrated attention (effect).

processing, systematic : the inner-workings or "through-put" result of systems; in *Systemology*, a method of applied spiritual technology used toward personal Self-Actualization; methods of selective directed attention, communicated language and associative imagery that increases personal control of the human condition.

realization : the clear perception of an understanding; a consideration or understanding on what is "actual"; to make "real" or give "reality" to so as to grant a property of "being-ness" or "being as it is"; the state or instance of coming to an *Awareness*; in *Systemology*, "gnosis" or true knowledge achieved during *systematic processing*; achievement of a new (or higher) cognition, true knowledge or perception of Self; a consideration of reality or assignment of meaning.

responsibility : the *ability* to *respond*; the extent of mobilizing *power* and *understanding* an individual maintains as *Awareness* to enact *change*; the proactive ability to *Self-direct* and make decisions independent of an outside authority.

Seeker : an individual on the *Pathway to Self-Honesty*; a practitioner of *Mardukite Systemology* or *Systemology Processing*, that is working toward *Spiritual Ascension*.

Self-actualization : bringing the full potential of the Human spirit into Reality; expressing full capabilities and creativeness of the *Alpha-Spirit*.

Self-determinism : the freedom to act, clear of external control or influence; the personal control of Will to direct intention.

Self-honesty : the basic or original *alpha* state of *being* and *knowing*; clear and present total *Awareness* of-and-as *Self*, in its most basic and true proactive expression of itself as *Spirit* or *I-AM*—free of artificial attachments, perceptive filters and other emotionally-reactive or mentally-conditioned programming imposed on the human condition by the systematized physical world; the ability to experience existence without judgment.

spiritual timeline : a continuous stream of moment-to-moment *Mental Images* (or a record of experiences) that defines the "past" of a spiritual being (or *Alpha-Spirit*) and which includes impressions (*imprints, &tc.*) from all life-incarnations and significant spiritual events the being has encountered; in Systemology, also "*backtrack.*"

Spheres of Existence : a series of *eight* concentric circles, rings or spheres (each larger than the former) that is overlaid onto the Standard Model of Beta-Existence to demonstrate the dynamic systems of existence extending out from the POV of Self (often as a "body") at the *First Sphere*; these are given in the basic eightfold systems as: *Self, Home/Family, Groups, Humanity, Life on Earth, Physical Universe, Spiritual Universe* and *Infinity-Divinity.*

Systemology : a modern tradition of applied religious philosophy and spiritual technology based on *Arcane Tablets* (in combination with *"general systemology"* and *"games theory"*) developed in the New Age underground by Joshua Free in 2011 as an advanced futurist extension of the *Mardukite Research Org.*

terminal (node) : a point, end, or mass, on a line; a connection point for closing an electric circuit, such as a post on a battery terminating at each end of its own systematic function; a point of connectivity with other points; in systems, a contact point of interaction; a point of interaction with other points.

turbulence : a quality or state of distortion or disturbance that creates irregularity of a flow or pattern; the quality or state of aberration on a line (such as ragged edges) or the emotional "turbulent feelings" attached to a particular flow or terminal node; a violent, haphazard or disharmonious commotion (such as in the ebb of gusts and lulls of wind action).

validation : a reinforcement of agreements or considerations as being "real."

viewpoint : see *"point-of-view" (POV).*

willingness : the state of conscious Self-determined ability and interest (directed attention) to *Be, Do* or *Have*; a Self-determined consideration to reach, face up to (*confront*) or manage some "mass" or energy; the extent to which an individual considers themselves able to participate, act or communicate along some line, to put attention or intention on the line, or to produce (create) an effect.

ZU : the ancient Sumerian cuneiform sign for the archaic verb—*"to know," "knowingness"* or *"awareness"*; in *Mardukite Zuism and Systemology*, the active energy/matter of the "Spiritual Universe" (AN) experienced as a *Lifeforce* or *consciousness* that imbues living forms extant in the "Physical Universe" (KI); *"Spiritual Life Energy"*; energy demonstrated by the WILL of an actualized *Alpha-Spirit* in the "Spiritual Universe" (AN), which impinges its *Awareness* into the Physical Universe (KI), animating/controlling *Life* for its experience of *beta-existence* along an individual Alpha-Spirit's personal *Identity-continuum*, called a *ZU-line*.

Zu-Line : a theoretical construct in *Mardukite Zuism and Systemology* demonstrating *Spiritual*

Life Energy (*ZU*) as a personal individual "continuum" of Awareness interacting with all Spheres of Existence on the Standard Model of Systemology; a spectrum of potential variations and interactions of a monistic continuum or singular *Spiritual Life Energy* demonstrated on the Standard Model; an energetic channel of potential POV and "locations" of Beingness, demonstrated in early Systemology materials as an individual Alpha-Spirit's personal *Identity- continuum*, potentially connecting *Awareness* of *Self* with "*Infinity*" simultaneous with all points considered in existence; a symbolic demonstration of the "*Life-line*" on which *Awareness (ZU)* extends from the direction of the "Spiritual Universe" (AN) in its true original *alpha state* through an entire possible range of activity resulting in its *beta state* and control of a *genetic-entity* occupying the *Physical Universe (KI)*.

Zu-Vision : the true and basic (*Alpha*) Point-of-View (perspective, POV) maintained by *Self* as *Alpha-Spirit* outside boundaries or considerations of the *Human Condition* and *exterior* to beta-existence reality agreements with the Physical Universe; a POV of Self *as* "a unit of Spiritual Awareness" that exists independent of a "body" and entrapment in a *Human Condition*; "spirit vision" in its truest sense.

253

Collector's Edition Hardcover

THE FUNDAMENTALS OF

SYSTEMOLOGY

A Basic Course developed by
Joshua Free

*collecting material of six lesson-booklets
together in one volume!*

"Being More Than Human"

"Realities in Agreement"

"Windows To Experience"

"Ancient Systemology"

"A History of Systemology"

"Systemology Processing"

All *six* lesson-booklets of the first official
Basic Course on Mardukite Systemology
are combined together in *one volume* as
"Fundamentals of Systemology."

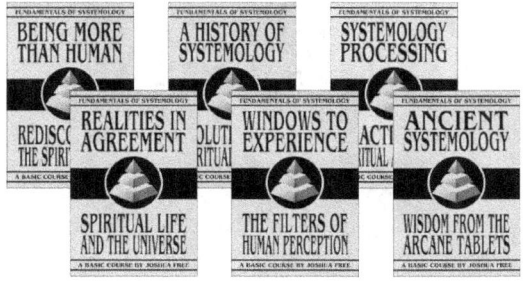

Lesson booklets are also available individually!

Collector's Edition Hardcover

THE PATHWAY TO
ASCENSION

The Systemology
Professional Course by
Joshua Free

All sixteen lessons available in two volumes!

"Increasing Awareness"

"Thought & Emotion"

"Clear Communication"

"Handling Humanity"

"Free Your Spirit"

"Escaping Spirit-Traps"

"Eliminating Barriers"

"Conquest of Illusion"

...and more!

All *sixteen* lesson-booklets of the newest *Professional Course* on Mardukite Systemology are combined together in *two volumes* as *"The Pathway to Ascension."*

Lesson booklets are also available individually!

THE SYSTEM

Seekers and students of the *Professional Course* and *Advanced Training Course* will also be interested in the original *Systemology Core Research Series*. These 8 volumes are a complete chronological record of *Mardukite NexGen New Thought* developments published by the *Systemology Society* from 2019 through 2023.

The Systemology Core series begins with the first professional publication released when our *Mardukite Systemology* emerged from the underground in 2019, with: *"The Tablets of Destiny Revelation."*

OLOGY CORE

The Tablets of Destiny Revelation:
*How Long-Lost Anunnaki Wisdom
Can Change the Fate of Humanity*

Crystal Clear: *Handbook for Seekers*

Metahuman Destinations (*2 volumes*)

Imaginomicon:
Approaching Gateways to Higher Universes

Way of the Wizard: *Utilitarian Systemology*

Systemology-180: *Fast-Track to Ascension*

Systemology Backtrack:
Reclaiming Spiritual Power & Past-Life Memory

PUBLISHED BY THE **JOSHUA FREE** IMPRINT REPRESENTING

The Mardukite Academy of Systemology

THE JOSHUA FREE IMPRINT
JFI PUBLICATIONS

MARDUKITE
ZUISM

mardukite.com